SO-AEH-524

for eating disorders

Mercy

for eating disorders

nancy
alcorn

Providence House Publishers
PROVIDENCE PUBLISHING CORPORATION
FRANKLIN, TENNESSEE

Copyright 2003 by Nancy Alcorn

All rights reserved. Written permission must be secured from the publisher to use or reproduce any part of this book, except for brief quotations in critical reviews or articles.

Printed in the United States of America

07   06   05   04   03   1   2   3   4   5

Library of Congress Catalog Card Number: 2002116168

ISBN: 1-57736-297-7

Scripture quotations marked "KJV" are taken from the Holy Bible, King James Version, Cambridge, 1769.

Scripture quotations marked "NKJV" are taken from the Holy Bible, New King James Version. Nashville, Tenn.: Thomas Nelson Publishers. Copyright © 1982. Used by permission. All rights reserved.

Scripture quotations marked "NIV" are taken from HOLY BIBLE, NEW INTER-NATIONAL VERSION®. Copyright © 1973, 1978, 1984 by International Bible Society. Used by permission of Zondervan Publishing House.

Scripture quotations marked "TLB" or "The Living Bible" are taken from The Living Bible ©1971 by Tyndale House Publishers, Inc. Used by permission. All right reserved.

Scripture quotations marked "AMP" are taken from The Amplified Bible, Old Testament ©1965, 1987 by the Zondervan Corporation and The Amplified New Testament © 1958, 1987 by The Lockman Foundation. Used by permission. All rights reserved.

Cover illustration © 2002, courtesy www.clipart.com
Cover design by Kelly Bainbridge and Gary Bozeman

PROVIDENCE HOUSE PUBLISHERS
an imprint of
Providence Publishing Corporation
238 Seaboard Lane • Franklin, Tennessee 37067
www.providencepubcorp.com
800-321-5692

To those who are

desperate for help

but feel there is no hope,

this book has been placed

in your *hands* for a reason—

it is no accident

that you are reading this even now.

My *prayer* is that you will read on,

because this book was written for you.

If you receive the message,

you will *never* be the same.

contents

——foreword by point of grace

Denise: Three years ago, God dropped in our hearts an idea for a conference for teenage girls where we could inspire them to lead Christ-centered, confident lives. We knew that Mercy Ministries, with its life-changing message of unconditional love, had to be a part, so we asked Nancy Alcorn to challenge the girls at the conference to make a total commitment to Christ. We wanted girls to hear the message of forgiveness and mercy to help prevent them from making choices that lead to life-controlling problems. As we were putting together the schedule, we saw a video clip of Laura from Mercy Ministries telling her story. We immediately knew that she had to be a part of Girls of Grace. At the first conference, she told her story to nine thousand teenage girls, and you could hear a pin drop. She was so transparent and honest, laying out her life so that these girls would not make the same choices she had made. As a result, many responded by asking for help. I believe you will experience the same impact by reading Laura's amazing story in this book.

Heather: While on tour and talking with fans, we hear many stories of girls struggling with eating disorders. Talk shows and magazines also discuss the magnitude of this problem in today's society. Unfortunately, few are able to offer real answers or hope for freedom. On the road, we often only hear the "before" of the story, and not the "after." This book contains amazing stories of girls who have had life-controlling eating disorders, and have come out on the other side. After you read these stories, you will understand that there is a way out—freedom is available in Christ.

Shelley: Working with Mercy Ministries has made us realize the tremendous need to help young girls learn to make the choices that keep them off a path of destruction. Now that I have a daughter of my own, I can't imagine watching her struggle with the devastation of an eating disorder. I pray that I never have to go through that, but to the parents who are, I am glad Mercy Ministries is offering real answers to a very real problem.

Terry: It's really hard to express what we feel in our hearts about Mercy Ministries and the lives that are being changed. It blows my mind when I hear a girl's story and then meet her in person, and see the dramatic changes. We have been involved with Mercy Ministries for years, and it never ceases to amaze me how God can change a life. In this book, Nancy Alcorn addresses life problems with solutions that are straight from the Word of God, and these solutions can completely turn your life around!

Over the years, the prevalence of eating disorders has steadily increased, causing many to search for answers—not only for the root causes, but also for the solutions to this growing epidemic. An often-asked question is "Why are eating disorders so prevalent now?" This issue has been explained as an evolution of self-medication that, in years past, manifested itself in alcoholism, then transformed into drug use in the seventies, and now is evident in eating disorders, along with the growing practice of self-mutilation (in the forms of cutting, burning, hitting, etc.). All of these issues that have plagued our society represent counterfeit solutions for dealing with pain.

Many women have been deeply wounded by incest, rape, physical and sexual child abuse, and other tragic experiences stemming from an unpleasant childhood. These women must deal with past hurts, be relieved of guilt, and work through the root causes. Extreme social issues, such as eating disorders, suicide, addictions, unplanned pregnancies, and sexual and physical abuse, are more than problems; they are symptoms of a deeper crisis—problems much deeper than what lies on the surface.

There are root causes in people that bring about the multiple social problems that we face today. We must deal with these root causes and not just the symptoms.

I spent the first eight years of my career working in government programs that looked good and sounded good on the surface, but the reality was that lives were not changed. During the first five years, I worked at a state-run juvenile detention center for girls with approximately three hundred beds. I saw hundreds of hurting teens with a multitude of problems. They were sentenced by juvenile court judges for a one-year stay, only to be returned to the same troubled environment they came from after their year of incarceration was completed.

Many of these girls ended up getting killed in street-gang fights, dying from drug overdoses, or taking their own lives. Others eventually ended up in prison. I continually saw broken, shattered lives and I knew there had to be a better way.

Even though I had a degree in psychology, I recognized that without a changed heart there was no such thing as a changed life. I also knew from personal experience that Jesus Christ is the only One who can heal a broken heart and bring true freedom.

It was during this time that I saw the need to establish privately funded programs that would allow the freedom to tell young girls they could be forgiven and receive new life in Christ, and that their past did not have to destroy their future.

Since opening the doors of Mercy Ministries of America in 1983, we have seen thousands of young women between the ages of thirteen and twenty-eight rescued from certain destruction. At Mercy, a willing heart and a sincere desire to change are the only requirements for entering the program and beginning the ultimate path to transformation. The girls who choose to come to our residential homes, with an average stay of six to nine months, receive care from trained professionals whose services are provided free of charge.

Since 1983, we have opened various residential facilities in the United States and abroad. The program combines God's unconditional love and healing with professional counsel and care, and the results are evident in the transformed lives of the girls.

Mercy Ministries, however, is not a quick fix. The girls are not miraculously "zapped" as they walk through the doors, never to experience problems again. It is going through the painful issues, not around them as they have in the past, that produces lasting change in the girls' lives. In the past, many of these girls would simply medicate themselves with drugs, alcohol, food, or sex, instead of dealing with the deep pain. At Mercy, the girls go through that pain, coming out on the other side fully restored.

The main reason Mercy is effective in helping girls is the Christian message of forgiveness and restoration. God doesn't just forgive but is able to provide a way for the shame, guilt, and fear to be removed. The key to freedom is not found in a particular program or home; freedom is found in realizing there is forgiveness in Christ and that your past does not have to control your future. The Christian message is the central theme, which includes support and a safe environment where the girls are allowed to be honest and share openly what they have done or what has been done to them without being judged. The Mercy staff is also trained not to be offended by the sins of the girls, but rather to create an atmosphere of unconditional love wherein what they have done is separated from who they are as individuals.

While many topics could be covered, the focus of this book is hope for those struggling with eating disorders. Perhaps you, or someone you know, is struggling with anorexia, bulimia, or binge eating. If you are, please know that you are not alone. You do not have an incurable disease, like some "experts" would say. There is hope. Healing is available. Freedom can be an experienced reality. You do not have to continue living in bondage, trapped in your own personal nightmare of hell on earth. It is possible for the chains that hold you captive to be broken and destroyed.

One of the current residents at Mercy Ministries, Heather, recently told us about her previous stay in a treatment facility for eating disorders. She knew she needed help, but she felt taken advantage of. She was being charged fifteen hundred dollars per day, and yet after several weeks, there was little progress or change.

About this time, Heather's roommate in the treatment center left abruptly, refusing all help, and a couple of weeks later, she was dead. This shook up Heather so much that she decided to search for another place that might be more effective in helping her. She found out about Mercy Ministries through a mutual family friend and made application to the program.

> You do not have to continue living in bondage, trapped in your own personal nightmare of hell on earth.

After being at Mercy for several months, Heather gave me the following note, hoping it would somehow be used in this book to encourage others:

I believe the book you are writing about eating disorders is going to be a life-changing book. It is so needed because there are few resources based on truth for those who struggle with eating disorders and their families.

Although I am sure you are aware of this passage of scripture, I felt a very strong prodding to share it with you, because it's been God's promise to me in my struggle with anorexia, and perhaps God might be able to use it for you in the process of writing your book:

They loathed all food and drew near the gates of death. Then they cried to the Lord in their trouble, and he saved them from their distress. He sent forth his word and healed them; he rescued them from the grave. Let them give thanks to the Lord for his unfailing love and his wonderful deeds for men (Ps. 107:18–21 NIV).

This is God's promise to me, and really for anyone who struggles with an eating disorder.

Read on, and get to know Laura in the first chapter as she bravely shares the intimate, heart-wrenching details of her intense struggle to save her own life. You will be amazed at the outcome of what looked like a certain path of destruction. Continue on to encounter more young girls who fought the same fight. These girls also won their battles, and so can you. Read on, and your life will never be the same.

one

Laura's story

before mercy

As I reflect on my past, many parts are blurry, and many are clear. The parts that are easiest to remember are the profoundly painful parts, and I remember them as if they were happening to someone else. It was like I had stepped out of my skin and could watch myself, similar to watching a movie. As I watched this movie of my past play out on the screen of my mind, many times I wanted to yell at the person I had become. I wanted to stop her, shake her very hard, and question her. I wanted to scream, "What are you doing?" and force her to change her lifestyle. The realization of these feelings instantly led me to know what my parents were experiencing at that time. It is a hard reality to face when you feel you have caused great amounts of pain and frustration in others' lives.

Have you ever watched a scary movie, knowing that the boogeyman is hiding behind the door? The young heroine is reaching for the doorknob, and as her arm extends, you yell, "Don't! Go the other way! Run! There is something scary behind that door!" I want to yell those very same words when I look back upon my high school years and view what became the beginning of a devastating eating disorder. I see the person I was and I want to yell, "Stop! There are other choices, other paths to follow! That path is horrible. Please, choose another one!" But at that time, I was unable to see any other choices. The pressures and situations I was dealing with in my life led me to one path, which at the start seemed harmless. Little did I know the life-controlling, all-consuming effects that path would have on me.

I don't remember the exact day I chose my eating disorder path. Perhaps the pressure to be thin was so inescapable that it seemed the path chose me instead. I do know that food had always been important to me, and I overate constantly. I was over two hundred pounds by eighth grade. I never drank, did drugs, or had sex. But I ate! While I don't remember when the obsession with food began, I do remember the first time I made myself vomit. It was messy and horrible, and afterward I swore to myself I would never do it again, yet knowing in my mind that I would.

THE NIGHTMARE OF SCHOOL

The summer before my junior year in high school, I was extremely unhappy. I had gained an enormous amount of weight and was beginning to feel that I no longer fit in with everyone else. I was involved and participating in school activities, but participation didn't mean enjoyment. I was academically successful but emotionally void. To adults, it must have seemed that I had everything together except my weight. I had perfect grades and perfect high school activities to complete the ideal resumé for college. But socially, I felt like an outcast. I had friends but not the close-knit circle of friends the popular students had. I didn't have a boyfriend because everyone knew that boys didn't date fat girls. I had started high school only slightly overweight, still believing that my personality was more important than my looks. I really didn't think I was fat or ugly, but other students quickly sent me the message that I was. Being teased was humiliating, and the more I hurt, the more I ate, until I had forgotten why I was eating in the first place.

Peers can be cruel, and my peers were no exception. In junior high, a teacher of mine started calling me "Chuckles" because of my bubbly personality and smile. This harmless nickname evolved into a cruel insult. My peers began calling me "Chunkles" instead of "Chuckles", and eventually it became "Chief Chunk." Walking down the hall brought "mooing" from other students. Some were rude enough to say to my face, "You are too fat to wear that outfit." I dropped my lunch one day and another student kicked it down the hall saying, "You don't need to eat that anyway."

Riding the bus was always a nightmare. I would miss the bus on purpose, just to avoid the embarrassment I faced every time I stepped onto the large, yellow vehicle. I had the unfortunate luck of being one of the very last stops before the bus proceeded to school. As a result, the bus was always full, and I could never find a willing soul who would dare move over to give me a seat. One boy would serenade me as I slowly made my way down the aisle of the bus. It was not a love song he crooned but a sick version of "I Get Around" by the Beach Boys. Instead of the phrase "I get around," he sang, "She's big and round, so big and round. She could squash the town, because she's big and round."

You may wonder where my parents were during this time. They tried to help, paying for diet programs, rewarding weight loss, and forcing me to exercise. This was all they knew how to do. They were acting out of love and concern. They were concerned for my health and wanted me to lose weight. How could they know that in less than a year they would still be concerned about my weight, but not because I was so heavy, but because I was so thin? Instead of diets, they would want me to eat.

That summer, my mom took me for an evaluation at a center for compulsive eaters. They recommended inpatient treatment for one month, and I was willing to go. I wanted to lose weight because I believed losing weight would solve all my problems. But our health insurance wouldn't pay for it, so I didn't go. I did, however, begin to see a counselor. Medication was recommended, but my parents were unable to admit that their daughter could be sick enough to need antidepressants.

> I wanted to lose weight because I believed losing weight would solve all my problems.

I began my junior year and continued to eat my way through the daily pressures. I was so unhappy. I couldn't concentrate, and all I thought about was my weight and how no one liked me because I was fat. I felt alone and unpopular—like a social outcast. These feelings began to interfere with my academic schoolwork. I couldn't concentrate on school. I began to fail my math class and dropped to a C in my history class.

PRESSURE FROM PARENTS

My entire life I had been an excellent student. In my household, the question was not "if" I would go to college but "where" I would go to college. Success was not an option; it was a demand. My father would inquire at the dinner table, "Are you getting all A's this semester?" A negative answer was not acceptable. He would also compare my perform-ance to my sister's. She had received two B's during her high school career and, as a result, was one percentage point too low in her class rank to receive a full scholarship to an award-winning school. My father constantly reminded me of this situation and encouraged me not to make the same mistake as my sister.

My father's motives to drive me to succeed were well-intentioned but misguided. When I understood his reasons, I felt a deeper bond with my father and realized his great love for me. But during high school, all I felt was pressure to be the best in everything, at any cost.

At this point, my memory begins to get a little fuzzy, and this is where I step out of my body and watch myself. I was seeing a counselor at this time and she had recommended a teen meeting of Overeaters Anonymous. My mother would drive me forty-five minutes to these meetings once a week. There, a group of adolescent girls would sit and talk about dieting, eating, laxative abuse, vomiting, and other destructive behaviors. An adult was not present to monitor the discussion. I am still not sure how these meetings were supposed to help me. But I faithfully attended and made quite a few friends there. One of the girls that I met eventually became my bingeing buddy. We would spend every dime that we had on food and then vomit. Our parents ended our friendship when we were caught shoplifting laxatives from the local grocery store.

THE STRUGGLE CONTINUES

I was beginning to see that to lose weight, all I needed were a few "tricks," and then I could be skinny. But the weight loss seemed far away and distant, and the unhappiness took over every area of my life. I was soon suicidal, seeing no point in continuing a life that was so painful and meaningless. I engaged in self-injurious behaviors, slicing my arms with knives and razors. I had learned about "cutting" in the group I was attending, and it seemed like an answer to some of the pain I was feeling. My counselor found out about it, and I was admitted to a psychiatric hospital that very same day. Luckily for me, or so it seemed at the time, I was placed on the eating disorders' unit, where I could continue to focus on food and dieting and learn more tricks to weight loss.

I don't remember much about my first stay on the eating disorders' unit, other than it was pretty useless. As I said, I did learn about vomiting and laxatives. I don't really remember what the therapy consisted of. I was placed on medication immediately after being admitted to the hospital. The pill in the morning caused sleeplessness, and the pill at night made me tired. I guess the doctor figured they would cancel out each other. We were all weighed every morning, in a hospital gown, with our backs turned to the scale. Our meals arrived, prepared for us by a dietician, and we had to eat the entire contents while being watched by a nurse. After a meal, we could not return to our rooms for two hours. Between the three meals and three snacks per day, we went to our rooms very little.

It always amazed me that on a unit where the staff is trying to teach you how to focus on your feelings and emotions rather than food, the main emphasis of every day was food. The constant chatter centered on when the trays would arrive, what nurse was eating with us, what would be served that day, how we could hide what we didn't want to eat, and how fat this food was going to make us. Ironically, at that point in my life, I did not think I had an eating disorder.

It is difficult to recall the exact order of the events of this time because of the medication I was given. Eventually it progressed to the point that I was on three or four different medications at a time, and my hands would shake as a result. This experience was painful, and as soon as it was over, I tried to forget about it. Now as I try to recall, the events seem misplaced and scattered.

I was overweight and used food as comfort, but my daily focus was not on food. My stay on the eating disorders' unit shifted that focus. Professionals told me that my eating disorder was about feelings and the inability to express them. But I saw an eating disorder as a logical way to solve my main problem in life—my weight. I was being tortured in school because of my size, so the logical solution was to conform to the standards of my school and become a socially accept-able size. It seemed rational to me.

All throughout the struggle with the eating disorder, people would tell me that what I was feeling was not factual or true. I knew that my father would not disown me if I got a B in school, but it felt true. My reality was based on my feelings and perceptions. I was often told that I was not fat, but in the mirror, I saw a fat person. If I looked in the mirror everyday and saw a fat person, am I going to believe that I'm not, simply because someone told me so? No. I was acting on my reality, and in my world the eating behavior was logical and made sense.

> I was often told
> that I
> was not fat,
> but in the mirror,
> I saw
> a fat person.

I returned to school at approximately the same weight in which I had entered the hospital. I rapidly began to lose weight as the year progressed. I never ate lunch at school and began bringing my breakfast to eat during my first period class. Breakfast consisted of a raw tomato or green pepper. I slept through many classes, too exhausted from the lack of nutrition to stay awake and focus. Teachers knew of the problem yet never commented. If any comments were made, it was on how great I looked or I was asked how I had managed to lose that much weight. Can you imagine the distress these questions brought? How do you answer a question from a teacher on how you lost so much weight? "Well, Mrs. Smith, I lost this weight by ingesting nothing but celery and coffee for the past three months. Would you like a copy of my diet plan?" I don't think that answer would have gone over too well. Why were they asking questions like that when they knew that I had an eating problem?

I started my junior year wearing a size twenty-six and ended the year in a size sixteen. Not one teacher warned me of the dangers of fast weight loss or questioned my methods. One teacher even commented cheerfully in my yearbook, "If you keep this up, we won't recognize you after the summer!"

My senior year is a blur. (I began to keep a journal the summer before my senior year, and entries are dispersed throughout the rest of my story.) The school was air-conditioned, and I would always be freezing in class. One teacher let me keep a blanket under my desk to cover up with when I got too chilled. This teacher would tell me, "You need to eat," and I would respond, "I can't."

BULIMIA

Even before school started, I had lost a lot of weight, and my body began to rebel. I could no longer survive on the few calories I was eating. It was then that the bingeing and purging began. This is a natural progression. A human body can only tolerate starvation for a period of time before you are forced to begin eating. The binges were small at first, just normal-sized meals, but progressed into evening-long marathons into grocery stores and all-you-can-eat buffets. I often wonder what the employees at these restaurants thought of me. I could eat more than a man twice my size, leave for the bathroom, return, and eat again. None of them ever commented, but they did look at me strangely. I learned to eat at self-serve restaurants to avoid the glances from strangers.

AM I CRAZY?

While I was starving myself, I didn't feel that anything was wrong with me. I was in control, just on a diet; no problem here. But when the bingeing began, something in my brain clicked, and I realized that I had a serious problem. How could I not be forced to face the fact that something was seriously wrong when I was spending time every day staring at my reflection in a pool of vomit in the bathroom toilet? Making myself throw up was not a pleasant experience, yet I continued to do it every day. It became automatic, just a normal part of the eating process. What goes in must come out. I also added laxatives to my new weight-loss plan. Laxatives are disgusting, no question about it. To this day, I get nauseous just thinking about swallowing a laxative. After taking an entire box of laxatives, I would be up the entire night with cramping and vomiting. I would be extremely dehydrated, but I felt thinner. At school

I would have to urgently leave in the middle of class and run to a bathroom, praying that I would make it to the stall in time.

LYING

Along with the bingeing and purging came a new ability to lie. I lied to my parents all the time. They were concerned and would question my eating habits, but I always lied. "Am I throwing up? Of course not, Mom! How can you think that?" All the while I would be praying, "Please let her believe me; please let her believe me."

> I just weighed myself on my sister's scale. AAAGGHHH! I have gained so much weight; tomorrow I have to get some laxatives and maybe some water pills too. Especially since I'm going on vacation Wednesday. I am really unhappy. I can't stand anything anymore. Nothing is fun anymore. I dread time because I don't know what is going to happen. I really am feeling stress about going back to school and going to college. I want it all to end. Especially my weight. I just threw up but I don't feel better because I ate that fast food Mexican stuff; I feel dirty and scummy and contaminated by it—I'll try not to worry.
>
> *Personal journal entry, August 1, 1993*

I was consumed by feelings of anxiety and dread. I would try to focus on school, friends, fun . . . but eventually it all returned to feelings of food, weight, and unhappiness. My life was revolving around the ability to binge, purge, and purchase laxatives.

Threw up two times today. Stayed up until 1:00 A.M. and binged while Mom and Dad slept. I was scared they would catch me but they didn't. I really want to lose a lot of weight. I need to look better. I feel like I've been fat forever and will never look good. Everyone looks at me and says "what a fatso" or "she's so ugly"— they never say it out loud but I know they think it. If only I could stop bingeing or stop eating entirely. I think I am going crazy. My mind is all jumbled, and I can't figure out what's going on. One minute I think I'm okay, and the next I am going to cry. I want everything to just stop so I won't have to deal with anything.

Personal journal entry, August 15, 1993

MAINTAINING THE "PERFECT IMAGE"

The school year continued with me bingeing and purging every day. I was sleeping in class, rushing to the bathroom because of laxatives, and crying at the drop of a hat. My hair was starting to fall out, and I had very little energy. I was still making straight A's and was president of the Key Club, a service organization.

know I hurt my mom. I thought I could get better. I get up in the morning, and I will think I look okay, but that thought is chased away by demons in my mind, and the good becomes as small as a grain of sand. Why am I so fat? Why can't I lose weight? Why do I always disappoint everyone—including myself? Does anyone understand? I don't know anymore. I am really confused and walking on eggshells. I don't want to confront Mom and Dad. I know I've hurt them. I wish they could understand that I don't do this on purpose to hurt them.

Personal journal entry, March 9, 1994

I knew that I was hurting my parents, but what I didn't realize was the damage I was causing myself. I knew I was in pain, but I had reached a point where I didn't think the pain would ever end. I didn't want to die, but I couldn't continue to live with the agony.

I lay here and I wonder—this is bizarre—Will they miss me if I die? Will they sit and watch tapes of me and cry or will they be like—oh, she was a pain in the butt anyhow. If they only knew how I really feel. Who am I? I don't know the true me—I am different for so many different people. Which one is me—the one most people like I guess. Every person I pretend to be is fat—so how could they like me? Am I psycho or what? Don't answer that! Just get in shape woman—

get yourself motivated—get up and do it—you can lose weight. Keep thinking these thoughts and I will!

Personal journal entry, March 31, 1994

I still thought that I could "whip myself into shape." I figured that if I could just muster the will power, that I could make all of this excruciating pain end. I didn't realize that is similar to thinking that I could have single-handedly stopped a runaway train. In my parents' eyes, I was a runaway train. I had turned into a person they didn't recognize. I don't think they realized that they were watching me die. Day by day, I was closer and closer to being a corpse, inflicting bodily harm on myself that could end up being irreversible. I still wanted to be thin, but it was more than that. The eating disorder had turned into my everything. My world was myself, my food, and my body. No one else existed in that small world. I still heard the comments and took the criticism, but I now felt alone and lost. Who could help me when I couldn't help myself?

Threw up once today. I wish I didn't feel like such a failure. I let everyone down. Even myself. Why can't I just try harder? If I put in more effort I could accomplish so much. Lonely, dark, despair, desperate? Words on a page—what do I feel? So confused that I really don't know. How can you love me when I don't even know who I am? Where am I going—will I fail? I can't even lose weight so how could I do anything else. Why is everyone so much skinnier than I am? I am a cow. Mooooo! If only I could lose weight. If only I was pretty. My whole life is "if onlys." Can it ever be anything else?

Personal journal entry, April 18, 1994

DOWNWARD SPIRAL

The downward spiral into the eating disorder continued throughout my senior year. I was extremely depressed and focused on food and weight. I turned in every assignment and got excellent grades, but my life was incomplete and empty. No one, or so it seemed, saw past the facade of a successful, smart, motivated young woman. My comments to teachers always focused on how I looked, how much weight I had lost, or the newest diet to hit the media. I was pale, sleeping through class, dizzy, blacking out, and continually losing weight. Through all of the problems, I graduated high school tied with three others for valedictorian.

I had given my life to Jesus at the age of fifteen at a weekend retreat. I knew that I needed God, but I had always thought that salvation simply meant that you weren't going to hell. I didn't know that the Holy Spirit could help you overcome. The summer before I left for college, I attended church camp and recommitted my life to the Lord. I was determined to go to college and be successful, despite what my parents or friends thought.

COLLEGE

My first semester of college was very difficult. The new freedom of dorm life led to increased bingeing and purging. My body was continuing to deteriorate, and one morning I went into the bathroom to take a shower and woke up on the bathroom floor covered in my own vomit. I had passed out for fifteen minutes, due to the forty-five laxatives I had swallowed the night before. I again entered treatment over the Christmas break. I saw a nutritionist and placed hopes of recovery in the meal plan I was given. Armed with the meal plan, I thought I could conquer school, not realizing that changing the outward behavior would not change my thoughts or my heart.

My college career became a never-ending cycle of therapists, doctors, and nutritionists. I switched schools twice, in the hopes of running from my problems. Most of the time, I looked successful. I was maintaining a 4.0 GPA, teaching Sunday school at a local church, and working a part-time job. But on the weekends, when my roommate would go home, I took the phone off the hook and binged and purged.

Eventually my facade cracked. I was forced to call 911 from my dorm room because of intense chest pain. When the ambulance took me to the hospital, I thought I was going to die, and honestly, I didn't really care if I did. I was scared, but not disappointed, when looking at the end of my life. I was given intravenous fluids and potassium to ward off the impending heart attack brought on by electrolyte imbalances. I dropped out of school because I couldn't get out of bed. I spent many months going in and out of the hospital for depression, suicide attempts, and the eating disorder. After trying fifteen different medications, the doctor suggested ECT (Electro-Convulsive Therapy), commonly known as "Shock Therapy." He sat across the table from me and said, "I don't know what to do with you." This is a scary statement coming from a psychiatrist who is supposed to help you. He told me to apply for disability because I was never going to be able to finish college. I also applied for Voc-Rehab, which is a program that pays for school for disabled individuals, and I qualified because I was considered mentally ill by the state.

> When the ambulance took me to the hospital, I thought I was going to die, and honestly, I didn't really care if I did.

I had six ECT treatments, and I remember little of that time period. Most of the information from that time comes from the hospital records that I have read and my parents' descriptions. I do remember continuing to binge and purge throughout the treatments, as it was the only lifestyle that I could remember how to function with.

AT DEATH'S DOOR

I knew that I was going to eventually die. I knew that the eating disorder would eventually shut down my body and I would lose my life. Every time I would vomit blood, I would wonder, "Will I die this time?" My heart would race and I would become clammy and breathless, as spots of black would race in front of my eyes. My electrolytes were out of balance, and my body was struggling to function. There was no question; I was on a path to death. No one told me that I could get off that path.

HOPE?

After six years of an eating disorder, I was ready for something different. I wanted to die, but I also wanted to live. I decided to let the part of me that wanted to live make decisions, and that part of me chose to apply to Mercy Ministries of America. Mercy Ministries was first introduced to me at a Point of Grace concert, and I tucked it into the back of my head, thinking that I would never need to go to a "troubled girls' home." Who wants to admit that they are so messed up that they need to go to a girls' home?

Years later, when I was reminded of Mercy, I knew it was the only place that could help. I received a newsletter in the mail that told the story of a young woman who had been set free from the bondage of bulimia. Set free! I had never seen the words set free and bulimia in the same sentence, let alone read a testimony of someone actually healed from the disorder. I felt hope rising

> I felt hope rising in my heart, and I decided to find out about this place called Mercy Ministries.

in my heart, and I decided to find out about this place called Mercy Ministries. That story convinced me to apply.

Afraid of dying, I was willing to try anything. I had already tried everything else! When I informed my counselor that I was interested in going to Mercy, the counselor told me that if I pursued that course of action, she would not see me anymore. This counselor told me that Mercy Ministries was not a reputable place because it wasn't a "treatment center." I had been treated by three separate nutritionists, four different hospitals, five different psychiatrists, and five separate counselors. At this point, I really didn't care what any of them thought.

My parents were skeptical, but after years of treatment and no improvement, they were willing for me to do anything. When I proposed the idea, they were scared of letting me go so far away, but in their hearts, they knew that if I did not do something soon, I was not going to live. I will never forget sitting with them in my living room, showing them the brochures and then watching their eyes widen as I told them what I was going to do. I know that they made many phone calls, behind my back, to check up on the program and assure themselves that they were placing their daughter in capable hands. But we knew I needed serious help. When we locked eyes, the unspoken communication confirmed that I was on the road to death, and if going to a home for six months was what it was going to take to change paths, I was going to do it.

With these apprehensions in mind, I filled out the application, did the phone interview, and gathered all the necessary medical information. I found out I was accepted and arranged a flight.

The day I flew to Nashville, my mother took me to the airport, and we both cried as we waited for the plane to board. We cried because we were going to be separated, but we also cried because we knew it was my last chance—my last chance for freedom and healing—my last chance for life. The next time I tried to kill myself, I would probably be successful. My mom was releasing me to Mercy Ministries because she knew if she didn't, she would lose me forever. It was the hardest thing I had ever done, leaving my family behind and heading to an unknown city in the hopes of healing. The plane made its descent into Nashville, and I watched the city unfold before me. I said a silent prayer to God, "Lord, please let this be the answer. Please let these people know how to help me. I am tired of searching and digging for help. I am tired and weary, and I can't do this anymore. Show me the answers." As I walked through the doors of Mercy, I knew. I had finished my search.

during mercy _____

Nancy: I'll never forget when Laura first walked through the doors of our Mercy home in Nashville, Tennessee. For Laura it was strange, yet for staff members, it was a sight we had witnessed hundreds of times before—a new girl walking in on her first day, having just arrived. We already knew a lot of Laura's story and much of what she had been through. Our application process is quite extensive, and we ask that all medical records and accounts of previous treatment and/or counseling be sent to us before acceptance into the program is finalized. Laura had cooperated fully with this process.

That first day when Laura walked through our doors, we could see the depression in her downcast look and the shame in her inability to make eye contact. Her slouched appearance sent us the message that she was broken, depressed, hurting, and miserable. Like many girls who come to us depressed, we knew it would be helpful for Laura to remain on medication until she could work through the inner issues that were actually causing the depression. We did everything we could to put Laura at ease those first few days, but it was obvious that she was extremely homesick, and she cried a lot at the beginning.

BEGINNING TO CHANGE

Laura: My first step was to actually believe that help was possible, that nothing was too hard for God and that He wanted to heal and restore me. This was not an easy step because I felt so much rejection that I secretly feared that God might reject me too. How could I trust God? Where had God been when the other kids were making fun of me? Where was God when I was hurting, alone, and wanting to die?

> Well. I'm confused. I know prayer works but I am having a hard time doing it. I get distracted, partly because I wonder why we pray. If God knows our hearts and our needs, why do we need to tell Him?

He hasn't seemed to be there before. I definitely feel like I fit in here now, and I'm not nearly as homesick, but it still is tough.

Personal journal entry, May 3, 1998

My counselor told me that God was there the whole time I was being hurt, but I initially had a hard time believing that. Eventually I came around and began to understand.

It was not God's intention for me to be hurt in the ways I was, but the other students had a free will. They could choose to say whatever hurtful words they wanted, just like I could choose to hurt people if I wanted. Unfortunately, people hurt other people all the time, but that does not mean God is the author of our pain.

Nancy: In James 1:17, we are told, "Every good gift and every perfect gift is from above, and comes down from the Father of lights, with whom there is no variation or shadow of turning" (NKJV). Laura's childhood experience of being continually mocked and ridiculed by her peers was very hurtful and actually robbed her of the joy of growing up with pleasant memories with friends. Rejection and emotional wounds are not what I would call "good and perfect gifts." If we will carefully judge our lives in the light of what God's Word really says, we will be able to lead people into the truth, and it is the truth that sets us free (John 8:32).

Jesus clearly tells us in John 10:10 in the Amplified Bible, "The thief comes only in order to steal and kill and destroy. I came that they may have life, and have it in abundance (to the full, till it overflows)."

> Once I made the choice to trust God, I finally realized that the promises in the Bible were true.

These two Scriptures are what we refer to at Mercy Ministries as "dividing Scriptures." In other words, we must help people see that God is love, His gifts are good, and that anything that comes to steal from us, to bring destruction, or to eventually kill us is not sent from God. Why? Because Jesus clearly states in this verse that these things are from the enemy, and that God's plan for us is to experience an abundant life that is filled to overflowing.

Laura: I began to realize that I could trust God. I will never forget when this truth became real to me. I was sitting in the classroom, looking up different Scriptures my counselor had given me. I read 1 Corinthians 1:9, and the words seemed to jump off the page. "God is faithful (reliable, trustworthy, and therefore ever true to His promise, and He can be depended on); by Him you were called into companionship and participation with His Son, Jesus Christ our Lord" (AMPLIFIED). Once I made the choice to trust God, I finally realized that the promises in the Bible were true. I could trust Him to take care of me when situations were rough and defend me when I was wrongfully persecuted. He became my strength when I didn't have any. I also realized that I could make choices in other areas of my life that would produce positive change.

Most of the professionals that I had worked with told me that I would struggle with the eating disorder for the rest of my life, always trying not to give in to the eating behaviors but never being free from the bondage of it.

I feel distant from God today. I wonder if I ate if I would feel closer to God. It is so hard to surrender. For so long I've had the comfort and destruction of my eating behavior. I want to stop. I want healing. I'm getting along really good with some of the other girls, but deep down inside I feel different, almost unsalvageable, like I'm too dirty to be liked. Do people really like me or are they just being nice?

Personal journal entry, May 7, 1998

When I came to Mercy, I was told that not only was I completely salvageable, but I could be free from the eating disorder. I did not have to live in bondage, because in Christ, all bondage is destroyed. Isaiah 61:1 and 2 Corinthians 5:17 say we can receive freedom and become a new creation when we receive Christ; old things pass away and all things become new. Not only did my counselor at Mercy share these truths with me, but she also told me that according to Deuteronomy 30:19 I could actually choose what I wanted: life or death, blessing or cursing. But to receive this life and blessing, my counselor pointed out that I must surrender my will to God and give Him control of my life. This is where my real battle was exposed—I wanted control.

COUNSELING

Nancy: I want to share portions of Laura's counseling process with you from the perspectives of both the staff at Mercy and Laura. Through this process, you will see the amazing change that God works in the girls as they learn to surrender their lives to Christ and allow Him to heal their wounds and set them free. You will see the pain and anguish of acknowledging faults, mistakes, and failures, and also the awesome victory and peace that comes from the removal of shame and guilt.

First session: The counselor noticed first of all Laura's great contradiction of purpose. For example, she was so desperate for help yet so set in her ways to control her environment and those around her. She was totally unwilling at this point to surrender her will and give up control. Laura was very fearful and panicked at the thought of losing control. She came across as a "know-it-all" yet whined about the condition of her life.

Laura: Today was my first counseling session with Sherry. It went well—I think. The counseling work is going to be hard because it is so different from what I'm used to. I know I can be healed—but it is going to be a painful process. Sometimes I crave a binge so bad! I want to stop purging but it is so hard! My whole body longs to do it. Many days I feel like I'm very messed up, like something is broken beyond being fixed. Other days I think that I could stop if I really tried hard enough. I just don't know if I am ready to give up control.

Personal journal entry, May 2, 1998

Second session: When Laura's counselor opened the session in prayer, asking for God's help and wisdom, Laura had a condescending attitude and finally said in a mocking way, "This is such a different way of counseling—I am used to therapy." The counselor addressed her attitude in a very direct way. She said, "This is not therapy but biblical counseling. Let me remind you that if therapy held the answers for you, you would be healed by now. No counselor or therapist can help apart from Christ, including the staff at Mercy Ministries."

Third session: Laura came in with an attitude that she was much more mature than the younger residents and not as "needy." Laura pointed out to her counselor that she felt the other girls were very prideful, manipulative, and deceitful. Laura was commended for being honest about her feelings, but her counselor pointed out to her that the very things she said about the other girls were also true about her, and that she should be careful about judging. She then shared with Laura what Romans 2:1 had to say on that subject. "You, therefore, have no excuse, you who pass judgment on someone else, for at whatever point you judge the other, you are condemning yourself, because you who pass judgment do the same things" (NIV).

> **Laura:** Today I got upset at some girls because they were making fun of a video I wanted to watch. I am so tired of the gossip and so many people being critical and judgmental of others. I try to keep my mouth shut, but it is hard! I feel like I am one of the more mature girls and it is hard for me to deal with some of the younger girls because I find myself being critical of their pettiness.
>
> *Personal journal entry, May 16, 1998*

Put on Your Battle Gear

Nancy: Before true freedom in Christ can be experienced, we must realize that we are in a spiritual war, and we have to learn to fight and win God's way. In 2 Corinthians 10:4–5 it says, "For the weapons of our warfare are not carnal but mighty in God for pulling down strongholds, casting down arguments and every high thing that exalts itself against the knowledge of God, bringing every thought

> I was ready to replace the lies with the truth— God's truth.

into captivity to the obedience of Christ." This Scripture describes exactly what Laura's counselor taught her to do: bring every thought captive that is contrary to the truth, pulling down the strongholds in her mind and replacing those thoughts with God's thoughts.

In doing this process over and over, saying aloud about herself what God says about her, Laura began to think about herself differently and see herself differently. In other words, instead of looking at her problem and identifying with that, she began continuously looking at her answer and identifying with who she is in Christ. As Laura spoke over herself what God's Word says, her old image of herself began to change on the inside, producing changes on the outside in every area of her life. In 2 Corinthians 3:16–18 it says, ". . . When one turns to the Lord, the veil is taken away (spiritual eyes are open). Now the Lord is the Spirit, and where the Spirit of the Lord is, there is liberty. But we all, with unveiled face, beholding as in a mirror the glory of the Lord, are being transformed into the same image from glory to glory, just as by the Spirit of the Lord" (NKJV). In the Amplified Bible, 2 Corinthians 3:16–18 is even more detailed,

> But whenever a person turns [in repentance] to the Lord, the veil is stripped off and taken away. Now the Lord is the Spirit, and where the Spirit of the Lord is, there is liberty (emancipation from bondage, freedom). And all of us, as with unveiled face, [because we] continued to behold [in the Word of God] as in a mirror the glory of the Lord, are constantly being transfigured into His very own image in ever increasing splendor and from one degree of glory to another; [for this comes] from the Lord [Who is] the Spirit.

NOT A QUICK FIX—IT'S A DAILY PROCESS

As you can see from Laura's story, our value and worth do not come from our outward appearance or the ability to meet standards set by others or ourselves.

Our value and worth must come from a personal relationship with God. Rather than walk in the masking that comes with the deceit of hiding the shame and the behavior, we must realize that God is the only answer to what is the truth about our identity. Building a relationship with God helps us to begin to see ourselves the way He sees us. Receiving a personal revelation of God's love for us will build up our self-esteem, acceptance, approval, and confidence.

Laura's freedom did not come as a result of one quick prayer or a quick fix, but rather a process of healing and transformation that took place over a period of time. In Psalm 119:130, we are told that the entrance of God's Word brings light. Laura's breakthrough came because of receiving, believing, and walking in the light.

Laura's counselor said that in the very next session, Laura herself began to backtrack and identify the triggers from her previous trip home. Laura was so excited that she could actually pinpoint the problem areas and choose to change her behavior that she began dancing in her chair and could hardly contain herself. Laura told her counselor that in all the years of therapy, she had no recollection of anyone ever helping her identify the triggers. She had been unable to pinpoint what set her off—what led her to bingeing and purging. Now she could identify these situations and react differently.

From this point on, Laura's healing process took off like a rocket. Now that she knew how to identify the enemy and "target" him with God's Word, she was able to walk in freedom and win the spiritual battles by bringing every thought captive, speaking God's Word, and using her God-given authority to enforce Satan's defeat in her life.

GRADUATION—IN MORE WAYS THAN ONE

Two months after Laura's breakthrough of learning to take thoughts captive, she graduated from the Mercy program after a six-month stay, free from all medication and free from the torment she had lived with all those years. She returned to college and finished her bachelor's degree in elementary and special education. Laura then decided to enter graduate school, and she completed her master's degree in special education in August of 2001.

Two weeks after receiving her master's degree, we hired Laura to be the director of education at our Mercy Ministries home in Nashville, the same home that she had graduated from in 1998. Yes, Laura had come full circle! She is a very bright, attractive, and confident young woman who is an invaluable asset to our staff. Laura knows that she is right in the center of God's plan and purpose for her life. She has a passion to help every girl who walks through our doors experience the same freedom in Christ that she is still enjoying to this very day.

after mercy ————————————

A CHANGED LIFE IS CHANGING LIVES

Laura: At first, it was strange being back. For one thing, my counselor when I was in the program is now my boss. And although it took an adjustment time for these new relationships, I know that I am totally in God's will. My love of teaching and similar experience of being at Mercy is important for bonding with the girls. There are so many great things about my job. One weekend a month I stay the entire weekend with the girls and get to spend some down-time with them. I also participate in recreation with them on a daily basis. But I think one of the coolest experiences is when they pass tests or fill out a college application—things that some thought that they would never do—and now they are doing them, and doing them well! The most important part is that the girls realize that I love them—I've been through what they're going through, and I get to watch God work in them every day!

In addition to working directly with the girls on a daily basis, I also go out and tell my story in public and private schools, colleges, youth meetings, churches, civic groups, and any place where I have the opportunity.

At the time of this writing, I am preparing to move to St. Louis, my hometown, to be on staff at our new Mercy Ministries home in that city. Yes, to the very city where the "experts" told me I could never finish school or function normally, to the very city where I was told to get on disability, I will be returning to tell my story over and over to all who will listen.

> I was set free from the eating disorder, taken off all medications, and healed of the root issues of rejection, shame, and inability to trust.

I was set free from the eating disorder, taken off all medications, and healed of the root issues of rejection, shame, and inability to trust. I had seen three different nutritionists, had been in four different hospitals, seen five different psychiatrists and five different counselors, but it only took one God to heal!

the

Beginning

of mercy

nancy's story _____

When I first began Mercy Ministries in 1983, I had no idea that we would eventually help hundreds of girls suffering from eating disorders. I also never dreamed that one day God would lead me to tell about my own struggle years ago with an eating disorder. However, I now realize that part of God's plan is for me to share my own path to freedom.

Not too long after I became a Christian, about the time I graduated from college, I very innocently and naively fell into the struggle of my life. I was very weight conscious, as most young girls are. One night I was invited to eat a meal with my pastor and his wife. The food was great, and I ate more than I should have. They had a meeting to attend that night, so I volunteered to do the dishes and clean their house for them while they were gone.

Because I had overeaten, I began feeling nauseated. I kept trying to clean the house, but that "throw-up" feeling would not leave me. I had a strong desire to please this couple by cleaning their house before they returned from their meeting, but my body wasn't cooperating. I wished that I hadn't eaten so much, but what could I do about it now? Finally, because that nauseous feeling would not go away, I went into the bathroom and positioned myself over the toilet, hoping to find relief. Much to my dismay, I wasn't throwing up, but I wasn't feeling better either. I finally decided that my only hope in completing the house cleaning that night was to make myself throw up, thus getting rid of the nausea, and then finishing what I had committed to do.

It was not premeditated on my part, but as soon as I "helped myself" out of my misery by vomiting on purpose, this profound thought hit my head, which, looking back on it, I have come to believe was a demonic voice. The voice inside my head said, "You can do this all the time, every single day, and in so doing, you can eat anything you want and totally control your weight. You can eat anything and everything, no limits, and then you can purge so you won't gain weight." Are you kidding me? No more dieting? I can eat *whatever* I want, *whenever* I want, and not gain weight? That sounded too good to be true! Yet, I bought into that lie, hook, line, and sinker.

> I lived in constant fear of gaining weight and it literally consumed me.

This innocent but naive surrender to a simple thought that "seemed right" almost did me in. In Proverbs 14:12, we are told that there is a way that "seems right," but the end of that way is death. Before long, I was purging several times a week. Eventually, as a result of abusing my body in this way, I had many physical problems such as severe constipation and extremely irregular menstrual cycles. Even worse than the physical problems were the constant and continuous thoughts of food I focused on every waking moment. I lived in constant fear of gaining weight and it literally consumed me.

The torment of this bondage was so severe that there were times I wished I could have died. However, because I had accepted Christ as my Savior, somehow I knew there was hope. The ironic thing is that Satan could not tempt me in the area of drugs or alcohol because my desires had changed since receiving Christ, and I wanted to please God. But because overeating was not recognized as one of the "major" sins, I felt like I was not in any serious danger. I was so wrong!

The five years that followed were the worst years of my life. I could separate myself from drugs and cigarettes, but I could not separate myself from food—I had to eat to live. Likewise, as a Christian, I wouldn't dare consider going out and getting high or getting drunk, but for some reason, abusing food did not seem to be that big of a deal. It turned out to be the biggest deal of my life!

During those five years, I experienced the most devastating, all-consuming, tormenting war of my life. Only through dealing with the root causes of this horrible captivity was I able to be set free. For me it was five years of hell. Had I known back then what I am writing to you in this book today, it would not have taken five years. Back then, eating disorders were not talked about like they are now. In fact, I didn't even know that what I was caught up in was called "bulimia." I was so ashamed that, for years, I never told anyone what I was going through. After all, I was supposed to have it all together. Not so! I did not seek counseling or professional help because I wasn't aware that it was available.

Because I stayed in the Word, renewed my mind to the truth, and cried out to God continuously, I was eventually set free and restored. However, it could have happened much sooner, but I didn't know who to talk to, who to turn to, or what to do.

That is why I am writing this book. I don't want anyone else to struggle for five years or more because no one is willing to talk about this issue. People need hope, and people need help, and people need to know that freedom is available *in Christ*.

My plan was never to reveal my story, especially in a book that could be read by everyone. In fact, when I first began this writing, I had not intended to tell my own story—only that of others. But the more I wrote, the more I realized that I needed to get this victory story out in the open, so here it is.

There are new beginnings available in Christ! There is no problem too hard for God! The choice is ours; it is up to us. Freedom is available for all who are willing to hear and to receive. As stated in Hebrews 4:7, "Today, if you hear his voice, do not harden your hearts" (NIV). Now, twenty years later, I am still free! Twenty years later, I have the opportunity to provide a place for girls who want to overcome! Twenty years later I am telling my story to all who will listen! Allow me now to share briefly how I came to recognize the need for a ministry like Mercy.

founding of mercy _____

I spent the first eight years of my career working for the State of Tennessee, helping with teen juveniles and investigating child abuse cases. I saw firsthand the inadequacy of these state-run programs to offer real transformation in the lives of troubled young women.

I knew that only Jesus could bring restoration to girls who were so desperately hurting, and I knew God was calling me to step out and do something about it.

In January 1983, I moved to Monroe, Louisiana, to start Mercy Ministries of America. Mercy Ministries is a home for troubled young girls ages thirteen to twenty-eight that are dealing with life-controlling issues. I wanted these young girls to experience the love and forgiveness of a changed heart and a changed life that I experienced when I accepted Christ as my Savior and understood what it meant to be forgiven. We established a well-rounded program based on Christian principles that includes counseling, education, life-skills training, and regular church attendance. We try to make the program effective in changing their lives while maintaining an enjoyable and fun atmosphere for the girls by providing activities that are normal for someone in their age group such as athletic events and occasional trips to the mall, concerts, and movies.

We even have contributors arrange for special outings such as a weekend at a large lake house with swimming and boating. One particular group planned an entire day of activities on a farm where they were able to fish and swim. Many times God really touches the girls in these recreational times just as much as in the structured counseling.

Mercy presently operates homes in the United States in Monroe, Louisiana; Nashville, Tennessee; and St. Louis, Missouri. Future U.S. locations include, but are not limited to, Seattle, Houston, Los Angeles, Oklahoma City, and Raleigh, North Carolina. We also have an existing home in Sydney, Australia, and our second Australian home will soon be ready to receive hurting girls. Plans are underway as well to establish homes in the United Kingdom and New Zealand.

TREATMENT OR TRANSFORMATION?

Through my experiences, I have found that secular forms of treatment are just that—treatment. However, they do not lead to transformation. There is a simple truth in God's Word that says whatever a person thinks and believes in her heart about herself will be the way she is. I have seen the reality of this statement played out in multitudes of young girls' lives over the years. They seek professional help through treatment centers, eating disorder clinics, and psychiatric facilities, and they are often told all the things they can never change.

Like Laura, they are placed on medication after medication and given psychiatric and medical evaluations over and over—all focusing on outward behavior and never getting to the issues of the heart. Then, when all else fails, perhaps shock treatment is the answer. In Laura's case, after shock treatment failed, the insurance money ran out, and the family's financial resources had been depleted. The "experts" then proclaimed they had done all they could do for her, and she just needed to get on disability because she would never be able to complete her education.

As you know from reading Laura's story, she now has a master's degree in education and is on our staff at Mercy Ministries, free from all medication and the eating disorder that once controlled her life.

Had Laura believed the "experts" that she spent thousands of dollars on, who told her not what she could do but what she couldn't do, her life would be crippled today, and she would be living on governmental support.

Apart from Christ, there is no such thing as a changed life. According to Jeremiah 29:11, only God can give us hope and a future. It is impossible to overcome without the Overcomer, and these "experts" rely on their own insight and understanding apart from

God. Secular programs and secular treatment centers cannot produce lasting changes in the lives of people apart from Christ. They cannot forgive sin. They cannot heal broken hearts and damaged emotions. They cannot restore shattered lives.

The "experts" may not admit it, but those who care and want to see results are frustrated by the futility of man's wisdom and methods and the lack of results they produce. Eventually, they have to say, "The problem is not curable, because, after all, if it were curable, wouldn't my expertise and wisdom be able to help you through?" Frustrated? Yes! Full of pride? Yes!

> Apart from Christ, there is no such thing as a changed life.

The apostle Paul wrote about this dilemma hundreds of years ago to the church at Corinth: "For it is written: 'I will destroy the wisdom of the wise; the intelligence of the intelligent I will frustrate.' Where is the wise man? Where is the scholar? Where is the philosopher of this age? Has not God made foolish the wisdom of the world?" (1 Cor. 1:19–20 NIV).

Someone once said that the definition of insanity is to keep doing the same things over and over, expecting different results. It seems to me that if families are being charged massive amounts of money, with little change, then perhaps the "experts" need to reconsider the madness of their methods.

Recently, a distraught mother of a fifteen-year-old girl called our office and started sharing her story. In the middle of explaining her struggle, she broke down sobbing on the phone. She shared that she was extremely frustrated because her daughter is struggling with a devastating eating disorder and is in need of serious help, but she can't afford the help that is being offered. She went on to say that she called the eating disorder treatment center that was highly recommended by her daughter's counselor. The minimum stay is sixty days, and the admission's department told her that the price tag for that sixty-day stay would be $86,400, and a large portion of that amount would be required up front. She broke down again because she didn't know what to do; she was desperate to help her daughter but did not have the money to do so. This mother was absolutely shocked when our staff told her that this was the average amount charged by eating disorder treatment centers across the country. Some facilities charge as much as $1,500 a day.

I took a break from writing this book to attend the graduation ceremony of one of our residents. When a girl completes the Mercy program, we have a graduation with family and friends present in which we honor and thank God for the changes He has brought about in the girl's life. We were privileged to graduate Amy this morning. Interestingly, prior to coming to Mercy Ministries, Amy had been to this same facility I mentioned for two months, and it cost her family one hundred thousand dollars.

Not long after she left this facility, Amy began starving herself and realized, once again, that she needed help—help that her family could not afford. Her parents did not have any more money to spend on treatment centers, as they had spent all of their retirement already, so she decided to come to Mercy Ministries because of our commitment to offer help to all girls free of charge. The only stipulation for Amy, as for all girls that come to Mercy, is that they themselves choose to come, are serious about getting help, and have a willing attitude. Amy knew that Mercy Ministries was her last hope, and that if she didn't get help, she was going to die. She walked in the doors weighing 78 pounds, with a vacant look in her eyes and a haunting fear of death that was almost tangible.

At her graduation, she stood before me, beautiful and radiant, with a bright countenance and a boldness for God that brought tears to my eyes. Her parents were there as well, amazed at the changes in their daughter, who now weighs a healthy 110 pounds and is so full of life. We were all deeply touched as Amy told her story of overcoming an eating disorder.

My name is Amy, and I've been here at Mercy Ministries for a year now. I came to Mercy completely broken. I had allowed an eating disorder to completely destroy my life, to the point that I couldn't even function; I couldn't even leave my house. I'd go to the doctor every other week, and he'd be surprised to see me alive. Basically I was preparing myself for death, and I believed that if God was going to help me, He was going to have to do something drastic. I remember coming home from college because I just couldn't take it anymore—I was just so sick. My parents and I knew that we needed to do something. It was then that God brought Mercy Ministries into my life. He took my brokenness—He really did, and He made me whole. It has been a long, hard road here. It has been the most difficult year of my life, but it has also been the best year I've ever had. I just thank God for making me into a beautiful woman—a beautiful woman of God! I no longer have to serve anything but Him.

In September, I'm going to a Christian university, and I cannot wait! I get to go to college knowing who I am and not having to find my identity in what other people think or what other people say. I can go to school knowing who I really am and enjoy my experience. Thank you for everything!

It breaks my heart when I think that Amy's parents spent their retirement on sixty days of treatment that did not bring lasting freedom. When I heard Amy's story, I immediately thought about the woman referred to in Luke 8:43–44: "Now a woman, having a flow of blood for twelve years, who had spent all her livelihood on physicians and could not be healed by any, came from behind and touched the border of His garment. And immediately her flow of blood stopped" (NKJV).

The remaining girls I will tell you about in this book are much like this woman with the issue of blood who spent everything she had trying to get help from many different physicians. However, it was only when she was touched by Jesus Christ, the Great Physician, that she was made whole. I urge you to trust Him completely. He loves you and wants the best for you! As the Scripture says:

> Do not put your trust in princes, nor in a son of man, in whom there is no help. His spirit departs, he returns to his earth; in that very day his plans perish. Happy is he who has the God of Jacob for his help, whose hope is in the Lord his God, who made heaven and earth, the sea, and all that is in them; who keeps truth forever, who executes justice for the oppressed, who gives food to the hungry. The Lord gives freedom to the prisoners (Ps. 146:3–7 NKJV).

Once again, should we not consider that the One who made us knows how to restore us? Read on now to hear more stories where He did just that.

three

Compelling journeys

journeys to mercy _____

The following stories are just a sampling of the many young girls that come to Mercy Ministries of America seeking freedom from an eating disorder. While the families, backgrounds, and ages of these girls are different, they shared one thing in common. They were all desperate for help with the eating disorder that was plaguing their bodies, minds, and spirits, and they all knew that they could not change in their own strength. Some, like Jenny, are caught in a cycle of bingeing and purging. Others are abusing laxatives and diuretics, like Laura, whom you've already read about. Some are like Lisa, eating to cover up the pain of sexual, physical, and emotional abuse. There are others who are underweight, wanting to eat, but finding it impossible, like Kristy. The pain beneath the eating disorder may be the same; the journey and struggle may be different. Every individual with an eating disorder is just that—an individual. But there are some common threads that weave these young women together— similar symptoms, similar emotions, and a similar cry of desperation.

Laura shared her story with you for one reason and one reason only: for hope to rise in your heart, that you also can be freed from this hellish inner prison. Freedom can be your reality. Why? Because it is a promise God has given.

Just like Laura, all the other young women I will tell you about in this chapter are now living in this freedom, enjoying their journeys, doing life well, and pursuing their dreams. This can be your victory story too, or the victory story of someone you love who is caught in this tormenting trap.

Whether you or someone you know is plagued with an eating disorder, please realize it is no accident that you picked up this book. In Acts 10:34, the Bible tells us that God does not show partiality to individuals. In other words, what God does for one person is available to every person who will receive it. We must go through the process and deal with the inner issues and the pain that those issues bring. Yes, healing is a process, and God wants to walk you through that process. Someone once said, "Winners never quit, and quitters never win." Don't quit! Don't give up! Don't give in! The battle rages and the struggle is real, but there is a light at the end of the tunnel. During my own personal struggle with bulimia, I related so strongly to Micah 7:8, "Rejoice not against me, O my enemy! When I fall, I shall arise; when I sit in darkness, the Lord shall be a light unto me" (AMP).

> In God there is hope.
> In God, there is a bright future awaiting you.

I can't even begin to count the number of times I failed, mainly because I was trying to win the battle in my own strength. But I didn't quit! Just like this verse in Micah says, "When I fall, I shall arise!" Don't you quit, either. Read on, because there are spiritual truths in this book that will bring lasting liberty and freedom.

In God there is hope. In God, there is a bright future awaiting you. He is the light at the end of the tunnel, and He is the light that is illuminating you right now, even as you sit in darkness. Walk toward that light . . . the tunnel does have an end, and you can find it just like these young women did.

KRISTY

Kristy's struggle was somewhat different than Laura's. You see, Kristy never binged or purged but restricted eating until she was at an extremely low and dangerous weight. Kristy is from Australia and the number of young women with eating disorders in that nation, as in the United States, is increasing at an alarming rate.

Kristy had experienced losing two people very close to her right around the time she was beginning high school. She lost an uncle to suicide and two months later lost her grandfather. Her family had difficulty grieving these losses, and Kristy watched as her mother and father were unable to cope with these deaths. Not long after that, a friend mentioned to Kristy that her legs were big, so she began cutting back on food. She began very gradually, and no one noticed the slight weight loss. Chocolate and fatty foods were cut from her diet, and she also began stretching and exercising more than usual.

Although Kristy was experiencing turmoil on the inside, she seemed to have it all together on the outside. She excelled in school and was awarded for her efforts. In fact, she was such a good student that her peers often called her a "square" or a "nerd."

The same year that Kristy began dieting, her parents' business took a downturn. Suddenly, Kristy began taking on more and more responsibility around the house, as her parents were tied up trying to salvage their business. She cooked, cleaned, and took care of her younger sister. Kristy had another sister, her twin, and this complicated matters even more.

Throughout her mother's pregnancy, her parents had not known that they were having twins. It was not discovered until Kristy arrived into the world eight minutes after her twin sister. Her entire life, Kristy believed the lie that her mother did not want her and that her mother loved her twin more. She was afraid to express her true personality because it was different from that of her twin's. Kristy believed that her family would only love and accept her if she were exactly like her sister. While these thoughts were not accurate, in Kristy's mind they were real. Instead of dwelling on these thoughts, Kristy focused on food and weight loss to ignore the feelings of depression and rejection inside her.

Her family began to notice the weight loss and commented on it. Kristy thought the comments would make her happy, but instead they made her feel worse. She had longed for attention from her parents, but now that she was receiving attention, she didn't want it. Her goal was to maintain peace in the family.

Avoiding confrontation was Kristy's desire, and losing weight brought on conflict with her parents. The more weight she lost, the worse she felt. The diet that began as a way to feel better about herself had turned into a monster that drained her of all energy and kept her mind in a whirlwind of racing, negative thoughts. Kristy was unable to concentrate on normal activities and worried all the time. Slowly, more and more foods were added to her "do not eat" list, and meals became smaller and smaller. Three years after Kristy began her "diet," she was admitted to a public hospital in Australia, weighing only seventy pounds.

> The diet that began as a way to feel better about herself had turned into a monster that drained her of all energy.

Kristy remained in the hospital for three and a half months. She gained weight, but her thought processes remained exactly the same. Her depression decreased somewhat; however, this was not a result of changing her thoughts but rather a physical response to the weight gain and slight restoration of health. As soon as Kristy went home, she returned to the exact same eating patterns as before.

Eight months later, Kristy was readmitted to the same hospital weighing seventy-five pounds. Kristy's health was in danger, and the hospital responded with strict rules and regulations. Kristy was required to eat everything put in front of her, including the foods she was extremely afraid of eating. If she did not gain one to two pounds per week, she was punished by not being allowed any visitors or phone calls and then put on bed rest. Even if she ate every single thing they gave her but did not gain weight, she was still punished.

Kristy was confused, as she had no remembrance of the hospital staff ever addressing her emotional or spiritual needs but only feeding her physical body. No one helped her conquer her fear of food or helped her process why she had begun dieting in the first place; they only focused on her gaining weight. Kristy felt betrayed by the staff, as she recalls their attitude being, "Fatten her up and kick her out!" To Kristy they seemed unequipped to handle the complex nature of anorexia and knew only how to treat the physical body. Kristy was not taught any balance; in fact, she insists that she was forced to eat amounts of food that were not normal or healthy in order to gain weight quickly. Guilt and self-hate consumed her, and when she left the hospital, she immediately began starving herself all over again.

At this point, Kristy's parents were at a loss, unsure of what to do to keep their daughter from killing herself with starvation. They looked for other treatment, but Kristy had already been in the public hospital, and the private hospitals were far too expensive. Her sisters were angry with Kristy, unable to comprehend why she was slowly committing suicide. Kristy was not sure why she was either, but only knew that she had become incapable of stopping the destructive behaviors on her own.

Her parents heard about Mercy Ministries, and although they were a twenty-four-hour plane ride away, they dared to hope that Mercy held the keys to unlocking their daughter's prison cell. The paperwork was immense, as Kristy had to obtain necessary visas and documents to reside in another country, but it was worth it. By this point, Kristy was so emaciated and fatigued that it was questionable whether or not her body could handle such a long flight. In fact, the airline would not take on the liability of Kristy flying without a physician's written statement. The doctors thought she could make it through, so with what little hope she had left, Kristy boarded a plane for the long flight to the United States. Her own strength had failed her, and she was now ready to look to someone who could help her overcome her losing battle with anorexia.

Kristy came to Mercy extremely underweight at seventy pounds and racked with fear. Fear gripped every area of her life and permeated every thought. She would cry after eating food—even foods like salad. When staff began to make her plate, she became upset because she had lost control of the situation. She had difficulty submitting to staff because of her previous experiences in the hospital. She felt that the staff were just trying to make her gain weight so they could kick her out of the program. Even though we assured her that this was not the case, she still seemed skeptical. Kristy viewed healthy amounts of food as "truckloads." She would eat, but she also cried throughout the duration of each meal.

A breakthrough came for Kristy when she made the conscious choice, "Yes, I am going to eat. I am not going to starve myself anymore." She began to enjoy food again. The power of Kristy's "I will" and "I choose" came as a major breakthrough. Kristy finally realized that she could make the choice to obey God and do the right thing, regardless of what her feelings and emotions were screaming at her. When the power of sin is broken over our lives through genuine repentance, we are free to choose, and Kristy began choosing life. "I call heaven and earth as witnesses today against you, that I have set before you life and death, blessing and cursing; therefore choose life, that both you and your descendants may live" (Deut. 30:19 NKJV).

At times, Kristy would try to win the battle in her own strength but without success. During these times she experienced a lot of guilt and condemnation, and she would also become physically tired. It was during the times of failure that Kristy learned what it means to run to God and receive His mercy in her time of need. She also learned that God is a very present help in the time of trouble. "For we do not have a High Priest who cannot sympathize with our weaknesses, but was in all points tempted as we are, yet without sin. Let us therefore come boldly to the throne of grace, that we may obtain mercy and find grace to help in time of need" (Heb. 4:15–16 NKJV). Also, "God is our refuge and strength, a very present help in trouble" (Ps. 46:1 NKJV).

Kristy also learned not to view correction as rejection. For much of her life, Kristy had tried to build walls to protect herself from others, especially specific family members who had hurt her in some way. She forgave these family members and also admitted to perceiving correction as rejection. These emotions were grounded in a desire to continually please everyone. She had to begin seeking to please God rather than pleasing others.

At times, Kristy would lose her focus. Instead of focusing on her healing, she would begin to think about graduation and life after Mercy. These thoughts would interfere with her counseling. She would have to pray and place her dependence on God, submitting to His timetable and relinquishing the reigns of her life to God, giving Him complete control.

After several confrontations, Kristy was able to admit that she was angry and that she was constantly trying to find ways to please the staff. We would point out to her when she was manipulative, and Kristy began to understand the importance of speaking the truth to others in love so that positive choices and changes could be made. Kristy and her counselor were able to discuss her thoughts prior to and after these instances and determine the factors leading to the manipulation. This behavior was stemming from Kristy's desire to maintain control and to avoid fear and rejection. Kristy would try to either recapture the past or ensure the future with her behavior. She began to see her motives in certain situations and slowly began to change the negative behavior to positive behavior.

Kristy also wore many masks. She would outwardly display love and kindness to others that wasn't real in her heart. She would busy herself with activities and planning all day in order to avoid developing relationships in which she could get hurt or rejected. It was difficult for Kristy to understand that others thought and responded differently than her.

Kristy was in the program over the Christmas holidays. During this time she had a phenomenal breakthrough in which God truly changed her. She was no longer easily offended, attention-seeking, or overly emotional. She gained a healthy amount of weight for her size, and her attitude was completely changed. Kristy began to look back and see what she used to be—a person with no opinions or ideas of her own who wanted to be safe, to fit in, to be accepted, and to be liked. She acknowledged that she was incapable of direct speech, feared disapproval, strived for more approval, and performed for others' acceptance and love. While these traits did not magically disappear, Kristy's ability to recognize them allowed her to begin to truly let God change her on the inside, thus producing outward changes.

> The eyes that were once dark, sunken, and hollow were now sparkling with life.

Kristy also began to learn about anger. She had been afraid to be angry because she thought it would make her a bad person. Kristy was able to practice verbalizing anger in appropriate ways to the other girls in the home.

Kristy also began to "catch" herself in negative thoughts. During a conversation, when her mind would begin to compare herself with others or negative thoughts would enter, she was able to "catch" the negative thought and replace it with a positive thought based on truth from God's Word. She acknowledged that, at times, she was her own worst enemy and that her expectations for herself were unrealistic. She began to seek God to know His plan for her future (Jer. 29:11).

There was no doubt that Kristy was healed of the hurts and wounds that led to the eating disorder, but we cautioned her that she would have to continue walking out that healing. She arranged to see a nutritionist, physician, and counselor back home in Australia to continue her healing process and to provide accountability.

Kristy left the program a completely different person. It was amazing to see someone so vibrant and alive who was literally near death weighing seventy pounds just a year earlier. When Kristy graduated, her weight was in the normal range for her age and height; however, the prominent change was in her countenance. The eyes that were once dark, sunken, and hollow were now sparkling with life. Yes, death had been swallowed up in victory once again!

LISA

Lisa has a very different story than Laura or Kristy. Lisa struggled not only with restricting, bingeing, and purging, but she also had serious drug and alcohol dependencies. By age sixteen, Lisa was a full-blown alcoholic, smoking pot daily, and doing LSD and cocaine. She smoked her first cigarette at age seven after her brother gave it to her. Lisa had a tumultuous childhood, with hurt and pain around every corner. Drugs and alcohol were ways to numb the horrendous memories that wracked her brain. When she finally became clean and sober after attending a detox treatment center, the out-of-control eating behaviors took over her life.

Lisa hated her childhood. Her entire life she tried to cover up the mess in her family, pretending that she had a loving family, a nice home, and a good brother. In reality, her parents were separated, her mother was physically and verbally abusive, and her brother abused her sexually. Her father never protected her from either her mother or her brother, so Lisa had no one in her life that she could trust or look to for support. The shame and guilt of the sexual abuse was so overwhelming that Lisa turned to drugs and food to attempt to numb her pain. Because of the rejection Lisa felt at home, she looked for acceptance with boys and began sleeping with anyone that came along. She became extremely depressed, starving herself and snorting cocaine.

Her mother had schizophrenia and, because of this illness, eventually gained 250 pounds. Lisa's mother would say extremely hateful things to Lisa, telling her that she was unwanted and calling her a slut. The mental illness became so severe that Lisa and her brother were forced to put their mother in a nursing home, where she later died of a massive heart attack related to her weight gain. When she died, Lisa's mom weighed around 400 pounds.

One of Lisa's biggest fears was that she would end up like her mom. She was afraid that she would become mentally unstable because her mother was, and she was petrified of gaining weight. She became obsessed with staying small, because she did not want to be large like her mom. This obsession was channeled into extreme over-exercising and purging. Her life began to revolve around food, and she was continuously purging throughout the day, often several times an hour.

While Lisa was able to overcome her addictions to drugs and alcohol, she could not stop obsessing about food. It was all she ever thought about. She knew she needed help but did not know where to turn. She had already been in several treatment centers for drug abuse and depression and had tried many antidepressants, but nothing had helped. The traumatic events that she had experienced as a child kept running through her mind, and the only way Lisa had found to control the thoughts was to binge and purge. If she continually focused on food, she did not have to think about anything else; Lisa could block the painful memories.

Lisa continued to spiral downward. She was losing more and more weight and began experiencing health problems because of the bingeing and purging. She couldn't keep a job because of her lack of focus and constant anxiety. Eventually she found a job as a nanny, but while the children were at school, she would binge and purge. Lisa would even steal from the family she worked for to buy food.

> No counselor or program can produce a changed heart—only Christ can do that.

She had given her life to Christ several years before, and it was through the power of God that she was able to overcome her drug and alcohol addictions. Lisa began to pray that God would bring something into her life that would help her with her eating disorder. She knew that all things were possible with God but needed someone to help her walk through the memories that were hidden by the bingeing and purging.

When Lisa found out about Mercy Ministries, she was amazed and knew that it was an answer to her prayers. Her life was out of control, and she knew she needed help. Because Lisa had been in other treatment centers for drugs and alcohol, she knew that the answer could not be found in only changing her behavior. Lisa wanted a heart change. No counselor or program can produce a changed heart—only Christ can do that. Deep down, Lisa knew this was her last chance.

Lisa said, "I just remember screaming out to God that if He was there, if He created me to be on this earth, and if He wouldn't let me die, then He has to help me live." She had been desperate, wanting to die, and even tried several times to commit suicide. This is how Lisa came to Mercy Ministries.

Lisa came ready to change but had a hard time doing so. At first, she desperately wanted to go home because she felt that she didn't fit in with the other girls and that she was being excluded. She soon realized that part of this she brought on herself because she was putting up walls by rolling her eyes and other such behavior. When she started to be real and vulnerable, then the other girls began reaching out to befriend her.

During the beginning of her stay, Lisa was throwing up every single day. She would feel unsatisfied with her meals and attempt to fill emotional needs with food. She would also feel unsatisfied because she was avoiding foods that she really liked because of their fat or calorie content. She would fill up on low-calorie bulk foods, like salads, and avoid her favorite foods. She would then feel unsatisfied, yet stuffed, and would purge. Lisa began losing weight and at one point became frustrated as she was getting ready for church and all of her clothes were too baggy and hung off of her. She began to cry and sob and throw clothes around the room. A staff member found her almost hysterical because she had realized how "grotesquely skinny" she really was. Now she can laugh about that moment, but it wasn't funny at the time. This was a breakthrough moment for Lisa because she realized that she had to make the choice to eat if she wanted to gain weight.

During conversation, Lisa was unfocused because of anxiety, frequently switching from one subject to another. Her desire to talk and sort through her feelings was real, but she had so many concerns that she would become anxious and try to cover all her issues at once. Her anxiety would manifest in hair twirling and biting her nails, even while she talked. Lisa even felt anxious about the way she prayed, wanting to pray "exactly right."

Lisa would say that she was "totally stressed out and overwhelmed" and wanted everything to be perfect. She was consumed with planning for tomorrow and was very anxious. She was meditating on negative thoughts that eventually led to a negative emotion and then to a negative behavior. She was taught 2 Corinthians 10:4–5, "For the weapons of our warfare are not carnal but mighty in God for pulling down strongholds, casting down arguments and every high thing that exalts itself against the knowledge of God, bringing every thought into captivity to the obedience of Christ" (NKJV). She was fighting with fleshly, earthly weapons, trying to control her negative thoughts with planning. She was even using purging to try and fight the anxious feelings. This verse helped her to realize that her fight is not in the flesh but is spiritual. She had the authority to take the thoughts captive and replace them with the Word of God. It was by His strength that she was able to choose to stop purging to cover her anxious emotions.

> She had the authority to take the thoughts captive and replace them with the Word of God.

Many more emotions rose to the surface when she finally made the decision to stop purging. Everything she had avoided feeling by purging rose up, and she began to feel even more anxious, overwhelmed, and depressed. Lisa learned to go to various staff when she was upset so that they would help her to have a right perspective. They would pray with her and help her to see God's truth of the situation. Slowly, she began to trust the girls and the staff, and as she used the Word of God as her weapon, the depression and anxiety began to lift. Her personality began to emerge from underneath the pain and brokenness. She was finally able to let the real Lisa shine through, and what surfaced was a fun, light-hearted, and encouraging person.

She worked through family issues and dealt with the emotions and hurts associated with her past experiences. She released to God the hurt, anger, pain, fear, frustration, and codependency issues. Lisa was able to make the connection that she viewed her heavenly Father as she viewed her earthly father. Her biological dad was impersonal, never satisfied, distant, unpredictable, untrustworthy, unreliable, and loved her based on her performance. These character traits had carried over into her belief about God. She began to realize that this was a distorted image and made the choice to trust God, even through the fear and discomfort.

Lisa also had to learn to set boundaries with her father. In the past, she had allowed her father to make decisions for her, and now that she was becoming emotionally healthy, she knew that it was time to begin making decisions for herself. She had to confront her dad and tell him that she was an adult and could make her own decisions.

Unlike Laura, Lisa did have past experiences of sexual abuse. This issue was difficult to deal with as the sexual abuse had led to feelings of low self-worth and loneliness. This loneliness led her to enter sexual relationships in search of acceptance and love. The feelings that resulted from the abuse also drove her to attempt to numb herself with bingeing and purging. She felt dirty, and eating and throwing up was a way to destroy her "dirty" body. She detested the sexual relationships she'd had, as they left her feeling dirty, used, and cheap, but she felt guilty about ending them because they provided the sense of love and acceptance she craved. Her counselor was able to show her how unfulfilling and damaging these relationships were and helped her to recognize the lies that had formed in her head about men. The sexual abuse had caused her to believe that she would never be able to have a normal relationship with a man and that she should have sex just to make people like her. She replaced these lies with the truth that God could heal her and bring balance into her life in that area. She began to trust that God would bring the man into her life that He wanted her to marry, and she committed to keep sex for marriage only and wait for God's timing.

Lisa graduated from Mercy after fourteen months. The girl that had been suicidal, anxious, depressed, and trapped in the bondage of an eating disorder was now free. She said, "I went to Drug Action, NA (Narcotics Anonymous), AA (Alcoholics Anonymous), the Answer Group, and the Recovery Group, still trying to fill this hole that was there, and I couldn't fill it." At Mercy Ministries, she had learned to let God fill the void, that His grace is sufficient for her (2 Cor. 12:9). She freely admits that her counselor had to "kick her butt" sometimes, and she loved that the staff at Mercy focused on the answer and not the problem.

After leaving Mercy, Lisa lived with two Christian roommates and got a job at the local YMCA working with children and sharing her testimony with others. She is very involved in her local church and has gone on several mission trips to other nations. At the time of this writing, Lisa is on a six-month-long trip working with YWAM (Youth With A Mission) in other nations, where she is undoubtedly telling others about the Jesus that saved her life.

A few days ago I received a postcard from Lisa sharing her latest news with the staff and me. Here are her comments:

> Hello! Just sending a note before I leave for Romania for six weeks. Working with street kids and really looking forward to seeing God move in and through us. I'm enjoying my time in YWAM and learning so much about missions. I'm definitely in my element! Hope all is well! Thank you for giving me financial support to help make this trip possible. I pray God will bless you because of it (Luke 6:38). Much love, Lisa Marie.

Lisa is a perfect example of the power of Christ to change a life . . . any life. If you need Him, call upon Him. He is a very present help in the time of trouble (Ps. 46:1).

JENNY

From the outside, Jenny's life looked perfect. She had grown up her whole life in a small town. She was popular, well-liked, pretty, and smart. She was involved in her church's youth group and even had her private pilot's license. But seething below the surface of her "perfect image" was a volcano of anxiety, pressure, and an eating disorder.

Jenny grew up in a typical home, spending time with her sisters, going camping with her parents, and spending every Sunday in church. But Jenny longed for attention, acceptance, and success. She felt that she had no purpose in life. Getting her private pilot's license had brought some happiness, and some attention from her father, but even that tremendous accomplishment did not fulfill a deep longing inside her. Her life felt out of control, and she responded by cutting back on her food intake and increasing her exercise. She lost some weight and figured that her life was set. She had great grades, looked good, and everyone was proud of her. Jenny thought approval meant that she was a success.

As she left for college, her doctor and parents suggested she gain some weight, but Jenny was not ready to give up the success she felt. And to Jenny, being successful meant being thin, having people become proud of you, and doing everything right.

She continued to lose weight and eventually had to give up her dream of being a professional pilot because of a surfacing medical problem, hypoglycemia, which caused her to be medically unfit to fly. While Jenny would never admit it, it was a relief when she was told she could not be a pilot because the flying was stressful and she felt extreme pressure to have perfect performances. Although she stopped flying, she did not lose anyone's approval because it was "not her fault."

One afternoon, Jenny ate a muffin and a mocha cappuccino and felt disgusted with herself. All she could think about was the number of calories she had eaten, how much weight she was going to gain, and how out of control she felt, so she made herself throw up. She realized that she had found the perfect solution. No one would gripe anymore about how little she was eating because she was going to start eating more—much more! Now she knew she could eat and throw up. And that is exactly what she did. She began throwing up all the time, eventually throwing up twenty times a day. She isolated herself from her friends and would not even answer the phone because it might interrupt her binge. Jenny finally confessed to her mom that she was bulimic, and her family decided that she would move home from college and get help. But Jenny wasn't ready for help. She enjoyed being thin and being in control.

When she came home, Jenny was miserable. No one understood her, and no one could help her. She started to feel even more out of control as her eating episodes increased. Her doctor recommended counseling, but Jenny had a hard time accepting what the counselor said. She wanted to act as though everything was fine, but on the inside she was falling apart. Her blood sugar was swinging from high to low, and her blood pressure had dropped to dangerous levels. She was finally able to admit that she needed help.

When she admitted she was ready, a friend told her about Mercy Ministries of America. This friend had heard a young woman speak at a college about her experience at Mercy Ministries. The young woman was a graduate of the Mercy program and shared how Mercy helped her get to the root of the eating disorder, and now she was actually enjoying her life and desiring to tell her story to help others. Jenny was encouraged by this testimony and realized that what God did for this young woman, He could also do for her. Even secondhand, Jenny was so encouraged by this girl's experience that she made application to enter the program at Mercy Ministries. Jenny was beginning to realize that perhaps God could help her through this, just as He had helped the girl she was told about. Since the Mercy program was offered free of charge, she decided to at least give it a try. What did she have to lose? It wasn't long before she too walked through the doors of Mercy Ministries.

Jenny entered Mercy Ministries excited and ready to get all that God had for her while she was in the program. Initially, she wanted to go home because she felt that God had already revealed a lot to her in the week she had been there. She felt that she could be more useful to God at home. The counselors assured her that God brought her to Mercy Ministries and that He had more in store for her than could possibly happen in one week. She had to be patient with His timing.

Jenny stopped purging when she came to Mercy, so she was careful not to overeat. She seemed to be very eager and willing to let the staff do whatever they felt was in her best interests. She was hungry to learn about God. She learned very quickly and moved through the counseling process at a faster pace than most. She began to experience freedom as she worked through forgiveness and breaking generational curses (more on this in chapter 4). She identified her ungodly beliefs and rewrote them as scriptural godly beliefs.

Jenny had to release to God the feelings of being unloved, not belonging, shame, guilt, and false responsibility. She began to be quiet and concentrate, instead of always thinking and strategizing. She began to set healthy boundaries with her family. She had a difficult time with this as her parents had always encouraged her to come to them when she was in need of anything. She learned to be more dependent on the Lord to meet her needs and not her parents. Her parents struggled with these boundaries as well. Jenny had to separate herself from her mother and realize that her mom's emotions were not hers. She had always catered to her mom's emotions in the past and felt responsible for her mom's happiness. The realization that Jenny could now pray for her mother and trust God to take care of her needs brought freedom.

> Jenny had to release to God the feelings of being unloved, not belonging, shame, guilt, and false responsibility.

Jenny also had to deal with the eating disorder and the way she had hurt herself. She dealt with the shame, fear of rejection and abandonment, humiliation, loneliness, guilt, turmoil, and chaos in her mind. She asked God to forgive her for the pain she had caused by manipulating others, and she forgave herself for the anger she had towards her parents, herself, and her sisters. By doing this, she received peace in her mind and heart (Phil. 4:7).

Jenny was very thorough in everything, always waiting on the Lord and displaying much patience in counseling. She didn't try to get ahead of God but tried to slow down and learn to just "be." She began to gain strength and walked more assured of God's great love for her. Her relationship with her family began to heal and grow. Her father was growing in the Lord, and her mother began reading a book about boundaries. Jenny's life began to speak loudly to her entire family, thus challenging them to receive God's healing and restoration for themselves.

Jenny needed to gain some weight to be healthy for her age and size, but she was not succeeding. She began to feel a bit restless at Mercy, wanting to rush through so she could graduate. However, her counselors knew she still had several issues to deal with, including feelings of unworthiness, shame, and judgment. She had not purged in a while, but these feelings were still surfacing. Jenny realized that she had not dealt with all the areas she needed to, including her family and the relationship with her mother. She was beginning to fall back into the trap of people pleasing, denial, and perfectionism. She desired to be totally submitted to God, caring only about what He thought and not what others thought. But, she still feared not living up to people's expectations. She realized that these were old thinking patterns and that it would take some time and practice to walk free from them.

While these feelings seemed like a setback, they actually brought about more healing. Jenny was able to realize that she had not dealt with all of the root issues of the eating disorder, even though a lot of freedom came from speaking her godly beliefs and releasing soul/spirit hurts. At first, Jenny was walking in deception. She had to be taught the difference between deception and faith. Deception is walking in denial, stuffing your true emotions, and glossing everything over. Faith is acknowledging or recognizing the problem and then speaking the Word of God over the situation to see a change. Jenny had a lot of denial about the relationship with her mother, and reading several good books on the subject opened her eyes. She had thought that her problems were brought on by her dad, but she realized that her mom had just as much to do with her problems as he did. She had learned from her mother how to minimize problems and manipulate. She was encouraged to develop a healthy relationship with her mother once she had seen some of the pitfalls of the past.

A true breakthrough for Jenny came when she realized how much the issue of control dominated her life. By listening to teaching tapes about complete surrender, she began to notice how much she wanted to control each event and situation in her life. When she released control completely to God, she was brighter, her countenance changed, and a load was lifted off her shoulders. She finally began to gain a little weight, as she trusted God to help her eat in a healthy way. More balance came into her life in other areas as well.

Jenny spent seven months at Mercy Ministries of America. She had willingly gained weight, learned to set boundaries, and was able to see that eating three meals a day could be healthy for her. She had grown in her relationship with God, and with the help of her counselor, Jenny learned to go directly to God for the answers she needed. Her counselor also spoke bluntly with her, which was what Jenny needed!

She returned to her hometown, became active in a local church, and reentered college to complete her degree. She began telling people about her struggle with an eating disorder and how she was set free. Jenny interned at her church, continued growing in her relationship with God, and also learned the "nuts and bolts" of working in a ministry. As her college graduation date was drawing closer, she wondered what God wanted her to do. Jenny began diligently seeking God's will about what she should do next.

Jenny had a desire to share her story and help others, but she wasn't sure what direction to take. After prayer, she felt like she should work at Mercy, so she gave me a call and asked me to pray about the possibility of working with us at Mercy. We didn't have a job right away, but I told her we would keep her in mind for the upcoming St. Louis home. She wanted to work with Mercy in any way possible, so she began volunteering her time, sharing about Mercy in St. Louis and assisting the marketing department in promoting the new home. Jenny even came to Nashville to meet with several of the staff members and shared her testimony with the girls.

I saw her quality of work and what she was capable of doing and knew that we had to have her on our staff. Her degree in marketing and her experience in ministry had equipped her to do whatever job we asked. I offered her a job, and she is now our regional development coordinator in St. Louis, helping get the word out about Mercy, gathering information, and raising funds. She is always willing to share her story with others who need the same help that she received, but it isn't her words that speak the loudest. Her life is a living example of God's ability to restore!

sharing the breakthroughs____

It is so exciting for me and my staff at Mercy to see these young women who were at one time so broken and wounded now out in the world telling their story so others who need hope will know that freedom is possible. In Romans 2:4 we are told that it is the goodness of God that leads people to repentance. These young women have experienced for themselves in a real and personal way just how good God really is! They now want everyone who is suffering from the pain and torment of an eating disorder to realize that Jesus shed His blood on the cross and paid a price for their freedom. He wants you to invite Him into your heart and commit your life to Him.

There is no such thing as a changed life without a changed heart. God will forgive our sins, mistakes, and failures and give us a brand new beginning! That's right! And not only do we receive a brand new beginning, but we also receive a new heart and a new spirit with new desires. We actually die to who we used to be, and we become that new person in Christ described in 2 Corinthians 5:17, with old things passed away and all things new!

ministry of multiplication_____

The four girls who graduated from Mercy that I have written about—Laura, Kristy, Lisa, and Jenny—all have one thing in common. They came to Mercy Ministries to receive help for an eating disorder that held them in bondage for years. Three of these girls are now involved in ministry, and they all share their story with others so that they too can know that there is complete freedom in Christ. In so doing, they are actually fulfilling 2 Corinthians 1:3–4, "Praise be to the God and Father of our Lord Jesus Christ, the Father of compassion and the God of all comfort, who comforts us in all our troubles, so that we can comfort those in any trouble with the comfort we ourselves have received from God" (NIV).

In Revelations 12:11, we are told that we over-come by the blood of the lamb and by the word of our testimony. These girls have overcome the enemy in their lives, and now they are helping others overcome as well. These young women are no longer identifying with their past, but they are identifying with the One who redeemed them from their past and made them new creatures in Christ Jesus! Just think, every person we help to be an overcomer in Christ can then go out and help others, and the ministry of Mercy continues multiplying into the lives of others. In other words, we get to be there for someone else, just like God was there for us.

journeys outside of mercy ____

I've told you the stories of these four girls who are graduates of Mercy. Now I want to tell you about three girls who *did not* come to Mercy Ministries to receive help. These three, as well as myself, have one thing in common with the others you have read about—they have been set free from an eating disorder that held them in bondage for years.

LISA RYAN

The first person I want to tell you about is Lisa Ryan, cohost of *The 700 Club* and former Miss California. Lisa struggled for years with an eating disorder before she experienced real freedom and healing in Christ. The divorce of her parents and loss of her brother had created deep wounds in Lisa's life, and to deal with the pain, she turned to controlling her image. The need to have a perfect Christian image led to a facade, acting as if her life were perfect, while in reality she felt out of control, angry, and insecure.

She was continually comparing herself to others and evaluating how she measured up. It wasn't until she gazed at Christ, through His Word, that she began to see and understand who she really was. She learned to be the best she could be with the gifts and attributes God had given her. By accepting her identity in Christ, Lisa no longer had to look, sound, or act like anyone else. She could be herself.

Lisa came to Mercy Ministries and shared her testimony with our girls and staff, proclaiming the freedom she had found by placing her identity in Christ. She also produced a special segment filmed at the Mercy home in Nashville, which featured testimonies of graduates from Mercy who have also overcome eating disorders. This segment was aired on *The 700 Club* broadcast, and as a result, we received numerous calls from young girls who "just happened" to see the program and were desperate for help.

> By accepting her identity in Christ, Lisa no longer had to look, sound, or act like anyone else.

Lisa is a special friend of Mercy and also a financial supporter. She authored a book in 2001 called *For Such a Time as This*. This book offers help to women who are caught in this deceptive trap, and Lisa sends ten percent of the proceeds from this book to Mercy Ministries because of her compassion and desire to see others set free.

DARLENE ZSCHECH

The second person I want to tell you about is greatly gifted by God in the area of music. Darlene is the worship pastor at Hills Christian Life Centre in Sydney, Australia. She has written and recorded many songs and worship CDs, but Darlene is perhaps best known for her song, "Shout to the Lord," that has been sung all around the world in many different languages and nations.

Like many others, I have known about Darlene for years and have been truly moved by her worship music CDs, but we didn't actually meet until 1999. When we did, there was an immediate heart-to-heart connection, but it wasn't until later that we fully understood why. Five years before we met, a friend of Darlene's from California sent her a copy of my first book, *Echoes of Mercy*. Darlene and her husband, Mark, both read the book and felt that one day God was going to use them to establish this same type of ministry in Australia. During this same time, I felt prompted by the Lord to begin praying for doors to open in Australia. God was preparing all of us years in advance!

Since the time of our first meeting in 1999, I have been to Australia thirteen times. Mercy Ministries Australia was officially established during the year 2000, and Mark and Darlene Zschech are the executive directors of Mercy there. We moved into our Sydney facilities in May 2001, and a second Australian home will open soon.

Through this process of working together, Mark and Darlene Zschech have become very close, personal friends of mine, and through our times of sharing as friends, Darlene revealed to me that she had struggled in her younger years with an eating disorder that she found impossible to overcome apart from Christ. It was only through her relationship with Jesus that she was able to break free from bulimia.

Darlene and Mark together are now overseeing Mercy Australia and taking in young girls who need to know that they too can overcome. Darlene is a constant example to the residents of Sydney. Her life speaks to them every single day!

SUE SEMRAU

The third person I want you to meet is a very dear friend who, in the past, has also overcome an eating disorder with God's help. At the time of this writing, Sue Semrau is beginning her sixth season as the head coach of women's basketball at Florida State University. Sue was named ACC Coach of the Year in 2001. She has a great job and a great life, but it hasn't always been that way.

Years ago, Sue battled with an eating disorder that was all-consuming and affected every area of her life. As a college athlete, Sue was all too familiar with the pressures related to perfection, performance, and meeting the high standards of success, especially those she placed on herself.

"It wasn't until after I accepted Jesus Christ as my Savior at a Fellowship of Christian Athletes camp that I began to understand that God is God over every area of our lives. There were underlying issues in my life that expressed themselves in inappropriate ways at inappropriate times. I thank God that He healed my damaged emotions and taught me to renew my mind through His Word and understand my new identity in Him." Sue Semrau has personally experienced the fact that we can only overcome life's problems when we begin to identify with who we are in Christ Jesus rather than continuing to identify with our problem, whatever it may be.

Working on a college campus gives Sue ample opportunities to share her story of being made new in Christ. She is now an accomplished speaker in the community and across the nation at various conferences, and she is also a popular speaker and active volunteer for Fellowship of Christian Athletes.

It is a great joy for me to have Sue as a personal friend and supporter of Mercy Ministries. Sue and her coaching staff have referred girls to Mercy Ministries who are desperate for help. They recently spent three days at Mercy speaking to our staff and girls, and I can honestly say our lives were impacted in a major way. Sue's story brought our girls hope, and they were greatly encouraged to hear how she overcame the eating disorder that once controlled her life and to see how far God has brought her.

the source of all freedom _____

In case you think that people must come to Mercy Ministries to be set free, they do not! In fact, we are sharing the principles from God's Word so that you can apply them to your own life, wherever you may be. Let me remind you that of the eight individuals I introduced you to that have been completely freed from all bondage of an eating disorder, only four of them actually went through the Mercy Ministries program—the other four did not.

So what is the answer? What is the one common element, whether in Mercy or out of Mercy, that these eight women all experienced? Each woman received Jesus as her Savior, and every one of them received a new heart and a new spirit with new desires. Each one received forgiveness for her past mistakes and experienced being a new person with a new beginning. These eight women renewed their minds to God's Word and began to identify with Christ and not with their problems. They found freedom in Christ, and you can too. A deeper look at some of these principles of freedom follows.

principles of
Freedom

focus on christ ————————

Too many times our focus is in the wrong place. Instead of looking at our problem and constantly identifying with it, we need to look at Christ and identify with Him and who we are in Him. When we do this, the power of God's Word creates a new image on the inside of us, and transformation begins to take place. As we behold Christ, we are changed into that very same image! The word "magnify" means to make big. Whenever we magnify our problems by continually speaking of them and our symptoms, we make them bigger and bigger in our lives, and eventually a stronghold of captivity is formed. That is why we are told in Psalm 34 to magnify the Lord and exalt His name. We are not to exalt our problem, but we are to exalt

His name. According to Philippians 2:9–10, the name of Jesus is above every other name that can be named, including the names of anorexia and bulimia!

> Our victory and power to overcome is in Christ and what He did for us on the cross.

Our victory and power to overcome is in Christ and what He did for us on the cross, which is described in Isaiah 53. Jesus defeated Satan for us, and we have been given authority. We have to use the authority of Jesus' name to enforce that defeat. Colossians 2:15 says about Christ, "Having disarmed principalities and powers, He made a public spectacle of them, triumphing over them in it" (NKJV). In Colossians 2:10 it says, "and you are complete in Him, who is the head of all principality and power" (NKJV).

According to this Scripture, there is no other way to be a complete person except to be "in Christ." As we speak God's Word over our lives and receive it into our hearts, that engrafted Word has the power and ability to transform our minds and our emotions (James 1:21). That is why we are told in Romans 12:2, "And do not be conformed to this world, but be transformed by the renewing of your mind, that you may prove what is that good and acceptable and perfect will of God" (NKJV).

deal with root issues ─────────

Many young women are free today because they were willing to believe God's Word, and they cooperated with God during the entire healing process. While replacing the lies (ungodly beliefs) with the truth of God's Word is an important part of the healing process, there are several other areas in which help is needed as well. There are four major ministry areas in the counseling model at Mercy, and every girl that comes to our homes works through these areas with her assigned individual counselor. However, using God's Word and applying His principles found in the following four areas can set *anyone* free.

UNGODLY BELIEFS—REPLACING LIES WITH TRUTH

As previously stated, one area we deal with in counseling is identifying the lies we believe about ourselves so that they can be replaced with truth. We refer to these lies as "ungodly beliefs" because they are things we believe about ourselves that are contrary to the way God views us. Please understand that this is a critical step to experiencing freedom. In chapter one, Laura's experience of identifying the lies she believed is explained.

This process is just that—a process. It takes time. If you will begin identifying the negative thoughts *you* are believing about yourself and start believing what *God* believes about you, you will begin to experience change on the inside. This can be done in a very practical way. Simply put, it is renewing your mind!

When you start to feel depressed, or have the urge to binge, purge, or engage in self-destructive behavior, start to journal the thoughts in your head. What are you thinking during this time? What statements are you buying into? It may sound something like this: "I am so fat and ugly. If I binge and purge, I will feel better. I must be crazy!"

These are lies and accusations about yourself that must be changed into positive thoughts! When these thoughts enter your mind, write them down and then search God's Word for the truth. It is not enough to simply not think these thoughts—you must aggressively replace the negative thoughts with God's truth. Find the scriptures that apply to your situation, and start to speak them over yourself on a daily basis.

Some paraphrased scriptures that would replace the lies listed above are:

"I am beautifully and wonderfully made. I will cry out to the Lord with my pain and He will set me free. God has not given me a spirit of fear, but of power, love, and a sound mind. God loves me and accepts me, just as I am."

Related Scriptures: *I praise you because I am fearfully and wonderfully made; your works are wonderful, I know that full well* (Psalm 139:14 NIV).

Now the Lord is the Spirit, and where the Spirit of the Lord is, there is freedom (2 Cor. 3:17 NIV).

For God did not give us a spirit of timidity (of cowardice, of craven and cringing and fawning fear), but [He has given us a spirit] of power and of love and of calm and well-balanced mind and discipline and self-control (2 Timothy 1:7 AMP).

As you begin to learn these scriptures, soon you will be able to quickly recognize thoughts that are negative and self-defeating and immediately replace them with positive truths from God's Word that counteract the negative lies. When the thought has been replaced, the urge to binge, purge, starve, etc., will begin to weaken.

You can renew your mind with the Word of God! Romans 12:2 states, "Do not conform any longer to the pattern of this world, but be transformed by the renewing of your mind. Then you will be able to test and approve what God's will is—his good, pleasing and perfect will" (NIV). Overcoming an eating disorder is not about simply stopping the behaviors, but it is about being changed on the inside, and this can only take place by renewing your mind. Identify the lies you are believing and then find out the truth of God's Word.

The lies Laura believed are listed in Appendix A, along with corresponding truth and scriptures. Please understand that these are Laura's negative thoughts and corresponding scriptures. It is important that each person identify the lies he or she believes and find corresponding scripture to replace those negative thoughts. Simply put, this is how to replace lies with truth!

GENERATIONAL SINS AND PATTERNS

Another area is that of generational sins and patterns in our families. When we receive Christ as our Savior, the curse is broken because He became a curse for us. Galatians 3:13 tells us, "Christ has redeemed us from the curse of the law, having become a curse for us (for it is written, 'Cursed is everyone who hangs on a tree')" (NKJV). Jesus actually took upon Himself the punishment that should have come to us. In reality, He took our place, suffered, and died so we could be free!

When we choose to receive all that Jesus did, the power of sin and the curse are broken over our lives, and now we have the power to choose to follow God's way. We can now establish new family patterns, which I like to refer to as "generational blessings." Our obedience to God can pave the way for future generations to benefit from our example.

In order to establish generational blessings, we must pray and break the power of generational sin using the authority that Jesus gave us. The first step is identifying patterns of sin in the past generations of your family (such as alcoholism, depression, divorce, etc.) and then, through a simple prayer, break those patterns. You are then free from them and can begin, through obedience, to establish healthy patterns and blessings for your own life and the generations that will come after you.

HURTS AND WOUNDS

We know that Jesus came to heal broken hearts. When we have been wounded and hurt by others, it is important that we forgive and let go of all bitterness. The Bible says that if we will not forgive others, that He cannot forgive us. Matthew 6:14 says, "For if you forgive men their trespasses, your heavenly Father will also forgive you" (NKJV). If we choose to forgive as an act of our will, out of obedience to God, we can experience God's forgiveness and then ask for healing in those areas where we have been wounded and hurt in our human soul and spirit.

> God can bring you peace and restoration from your hurts and wounds if you invite Him into your circumstances.

By allowing the Holy Spirit to bring to your mind past hurts, you can ask Him to show you the truth of the situation. Many times the Holy Spirit may show you that it was not your fault, that you were not to blame. God may reveal during this prayer time that He was protecting you from even greater harm. In whatever way He chooses to do it, God can bring you peace and restoration from your hurts and wounds if you invite Him into your circumstances.

For example, when Laura was in her counseling process, she had many hurts in her heart from past experiences. One of the hurts was from her father. Her dad put a great deal of pressure on her, expecting perfection. Laura felt that she could never measure up and was deeply wounded from the rejection she felt from her father. She went to the Lord in prayer and poured out all her feelings of rejection and loneliness. Laura told God exactly how she felt and released the situation to Him. She then asked the Lord to heal the hurt, and He began to show her times when her dad was loving and kind. Suddenly Laura remembered what her dad would say about his childhood, and she realized that he was pressuring her out of a desire for her to be successful. He had not been encouraged to work hard and, as a result, felt that he had not done as well as he could have. He wanted Laura to do her best, so he had pushed her very hard. God showed Laura that her father's intentions were good but that he had just made some mistakes in the way he encouraged her. Laura was able to forgive her father, and the pain associated with the memory was gone.

DEMONIC INFLUENCE OR OPPRESSION

An additional area with which we help our girls in prayer and counseling is to identify any area in their lives where there may be demonic influence or oppression. For example, if an individual has been involved in pornography, then the door to demonic influence has been opened in that person's life through his or her own choice of sin and disobedience. In other words, demonic influence and oppression cannot just jump on us and gain entrance into our lives without our willful participation. If we have opened a door to the enemy, we must do what it says in 1 John 1:9, "If we confess our sins, he is faithful and just and will forgive us our sins and purify us from all unrighteousness" (NIV).

Once we have confessed our sin and received forgiveness and cleansing, then we can pray and exercise our authority as believers to break the power of any demonic influence or control over our lives. Why is that? Because when we ask for forgiveness and make a conscious choice to turn from that sin, the enemy no longer has a right to torment and oppress us because the open door has been closed through confession and repentance (which means to turn around and go a different way).

For example, most people with eating disorders deal with a lot of fear. They may fear rejection, losing control, gaining weight, or what others think. By looking up fear in the Bible, we discover many verses that tell us that as believers, we do not have to live a life of fear. 2 Timothy 1:7 says, "For God has not given us a spirit of fear, but of power and of love and of a sound mind" (NKJV). We also see in 1 John 4:18, "There is no fear in love; but perfect love casts out fear, because fear involves torment" (NKJV). Living with fear is living a life of torment. Using the authority given by Christ, a believer can close the doors to fear and live free of this torment.

How do I do this? All it takes is prayer. Say a prayer like this:

> Lord, You have said in Your Word that You have not given me a spirit of fear but of power, love, and a sound mind. I know that if You have not given me the fear, then I do not have to live with and accept it. I choose to close the door to the enemy, and I command the fear to leave me in the name of Jesus. Your love is perfect, and You have said that perfect love casts out fear. Because I have received Jesus Christ, who is perfect love, I will no longer allow fear to rule me.

God is calling you—He wants you to know that He cares, and He is willing to meet you right where you are, right in the middle of your mess. Allow Him to reveal the root causes and the core issues of why you are where you are today—He loves you too much to leave you there. Just like He did for me, He will heal you, deliver you, restore you, and bring you into your destiny. He is calling you—why don't you open the door to your heart? In Revelation 3:20, Jesus says, "Behold, I stand at the door and knock. If anyone hears My voice and opens the door, I will come in to Him and dine with him and he with Me" (NKJV).

Someone is knocking at the door of your heart right now. Why don't you answer? Your future depends on it!

about the
Ministry
of mercy

Imagine knowing for the first time that you are loved unconditionally—forgiven no matter what you have done—and special in the eyes of God.

From the moment a girl walks into one of the beautiful Mercy homes, her transformation begins. An overwhelming sense of peace and acceptance is felt the moment she enters the doors. She has come to Mercy because of a sincere desire to set a new course for her life. Mercy provides the opportunity for that life-transforming process by encouraging her to experience the love and forgiveness of Jesus Christ.

Unfortunately, not all girls that come to Mercy experience transformation. Some girls come to Mercy with a desire to change, but it is up to them to choose to complete the program, work through their issues, and go through the process of being healed and restored, giving the process the time that it takes.

> In God's way, if you want to find your life, you have to lose it.

One example I can give you of what sometimes happens is one girl, who came to Mercy with a severe alcohol and drug problem, along with a devastating eating disorder. During her time at Mercy she was able to overcome her problems with addictions, but she had such a need to be in control that she refused to take the initial practical steps that would help her eliminate her other problem. She worked through the addictions, but concerning the eating disorder, she continued on in the same behavior as before she came into the program. She refused counsel and stole food from the kitchen on a daily basis. It was not uncommon for staff to find vomit in her shoes hidden in the back of her closet. Because of the severity of her problem, we gave her numerous opportunities to choose a different path, but she absolutely refused and eventually confessed that she had absolutely no intention of ever letting go of it. The eating disorder was the one thing she had control of in her life, and she didn't want to give up control. She eventually chose to leave the program, and since that time this girl has lived on the streets. She has bounced from one detox center to another, been arrested and jailed, tried numerous programs, and still refuses to deal with that issue. As long as she continues to hold onto the eating disorder, it is hers to keep. God offers hope and a future to everyone, but it is up to each person whether or not she will decide to walk it out and go through the process and time needed for healing.

Not all endings are happy since change takes work and can be a painful process. Complete surrender of our will to God's will is required. It doesn't make sense in the world's way of thinking, but in God's way, if you want to find your life, you have to lose it. Unfortunately, not every girl is able to give up the control they think will bring them happiness.

areas of mercy _____

COUNSELING

As each girl begins her path to a new life, working closely with her counselor is critical. Knowing that she has come completely free of charge is one of the first steps in building a bridge of trust between her and the staff. Many girls have already been to programs that cost up to fifteen hundred dollars a day, with little or no results. Each girl needs to know that this program is about changing lives—not about making money. Biblical counseling and spiritual growth are the core of each girl's time at Mercy. All staff are highly trained professionals and specialists in their fields. Above all, they are committed to helping each girl restore hope and stability to her life.

EDUCATION

As girls look toward the future, the education needed to fulfill their goals is provided. Many girls entering the Mercy program are in the process of completing their high school educations. They can continue their education while at Mercy, using a home school program or correspondence courses. All schoolwork is supervised by trained, professional staff. Other girls have dropped out of high school and want to complete their diploma. GED preparation and testing are provided so the girls can enter college or gain employment when they leave Mercy. Girls preparing to enter college are provided with preparation for college entrance exams and assistance in the college application process. Individual tutoring is available when needed. The staff at Mercy Ministries is dedicated to providing the girls with the skills and education necessary to accomplish the goals they have for the future.

LIFE-SKILLS TRAINING

Once a girl enters the program, she soon discovers that the structure is very beneficial to her self-worth and an important aid in her healing process. Each girl is assigned household duties. Class time, Bible study, praise and worship, and prayer are an integral part of her day. Parenting classes are provided if she is pregnant and chooses to parent, and adoption services are available if she chooses to place her child. She also receives instruction in budget and finance, fitness, and health. At Mercy, each girl's restoration process is designed for her personally, according to the severity of her problems, but the approach to her restoration is the same—to promote spiritual stability by demonstrating and teaching the unconditional love and mercy of God, combined with the practical application and training she needs to live a victorious life.

GRADUATION

After she has completed her time at Mercy, freed from her past, she is ready to step into life as a new creation.

She has learned the importance of applying God's Word to her daily life and holding on to His promises during the tough times. Above all, she knows that she is not merely "recovered" but "totally transformed," a new creation in Christ. As each girl moves toward completion of the program, she receives education and career counseling. A special graduation ceremony is held with Mercy staff and her family in attendance. Many tears are shed as parents, grandparents, siblings, and friends replace their frustration and sorrow with relief, joy, and pride in witnessing the new life that stands before them.

a day at mercy _____

Following is the typical daily schedule at the Mercy homes:

7:00 A.M.	Wake up
7:00–9:00	Breakfast, Showers, Work Details
9:00–9:30	Bible Reading
9:30–9:35	Break
9:35–10:20*	Praise, Worship, and Prayer Time
10:20–10:30	Break
10:30–11:30	Class
11:30–1:15	Lunch and Clean Up
1:15–3:30	Recreation (Activities Vary)
1:30–4:30**	Counseling Sessions

3:30–5:00	School (For School-Age Residents)
5:00–6:00	Dinner and Clean Up
6:00–7:00	Free Time
7:00–8:00	Class
8:00–8:45	Study Hall, Group Prayer
8:45–10:00	Free Time
10:00–10:30	Quiet Time
10:30 P.M.	Lights Out

On Fridays, group counseling replaces praise and worship and class time, and a group outing replaces recreation.

**Counseling sessions preempt regular schedule and vary accordingly with each girl.*

additional information

God led me to do three specific things to insure His blessings on the ministry: (1) to take in girls free of charge, (2) to always give at least ten percent of all Mercy Ministries' donations to other Christian organizations and ministries, and (3) to never accept any state or federal funding.

Mercy Ministries provides help free of charge so the girls can fully trust the staff and know that the ministry is not trying to make money from their struggles and heartbreak.

Mercy gives ten percent to other ministries because it is a biblical principle of tithing. As you give the tithe to God, He will open up the windows of heaven and pour out a blessing so great you won't have room to contain it (Mal. 3:10).

Finally, I knew that if any money were accepted from the state or federal government, the ability to preach the Word of God could be compromised, and true healing and restoration would not be possible.

As Mercy has faithfully followed these three principles, God has faithfully provided for every need of the ministry, just as He promised.

Similarly, the Mercy staff and I maintain a clear vision of the ministry's purpose. Through experience, we have learned that God has not equipped the government to set the captives free, but as Luke 4:18 states, He has called us as Christians to heal the brokenhearted and proclaim liberty to the captives. It is our belief that if we provide places free of charge where girls can come and receive new life through Jesus Christ, as well as professional training in other areas, their lives will never be the same!

Mercy Ministries is supported entirely through contributions from concerned individuals, churches, corporations, civic groups, and foundations. Unfortunately, Mercy Ministries has limitations. Our biggest challenge is the need for additional accommodations to meet the ever-increasing demand for help.

You can join us in transforming more lives. Contact Mercy to find out how you can help provide a loving environment where mercy triumphs over judgment and broken lives are restored.

Please visit our website at www.mercyministries.com to request the following information:

- An application for a girl who needs help
- An application for adoption
- To become a financial partner
- To order teaching tapes, videos, or books
- To take a virtual tour of our home in Nashville, Tennessee
- All other inquiries

For those who prefer to write or call:

Mercy Ministries of America
P.O. Box 111060
Nashville, TN 37222-1060
(615) 831-6987

additional

Keys

to freedom

Maybe you're one who has asked yourself, "How did I get here?" "How did my daughter get here?" or, "How do I prevent my friends and family from falling into these traps?" "Where do I go from here?" Maybe you see the stories in the previous chapters describing your loved one, and you ask yourself, "How do I help?"

The first chapters of this book gave you glimpses into real-life struggles with this very real bondage of eating disorders and the freedom that is available through Jesus Christ. In this next chapter, we (the staff of Mercy Ministries) want to provide further information from our perspective on eating disorders and parental involvement. First, we want to guide you into many of the signs, symptoms, behaviors, medical consequences, and factors or root causes of eating disorders. Realizing the sobering truth about the consequences of eating disorders can aid in prevention, as well as the critical decision to seek help.

Secondly is a part specifically for parents. This includes information on family dynamics, with words specific to both fathers and mothers; the importance of leading by example; the dos and don'ts of communication; the significance of building self-esteem in children; the steps to take if your child has an eating disorder; and prayers and declarations for your child.

Although we do not feel that we are the exhaustive source of solutions for eating disorders, we have learned that the principles of Proverbs 3:5–6 give us direction for everyone we help: "Trust in the Lord with all your heart, and lean not on your own understanding, in all your ways acknowledge Him, and He shall direct your paths" (NKJV).

signs and symptoms _____

Many children and teenagers can exhibit one or more of the following signs, symptoms, and behaviors for any number of reasons. This DOES NOT necessarily mean that your child has an eating disorder!

However, many people suffering from an eating disorder may exhibit signs of more than one and may vacillate between one eating disorder and another.

ANOREXIA NERVOSA

- Intense fear of gaining weight
- Is already thin and weight is dropping
- Cessation of menstrual cycle for three consecutive cycles
- Counts every calorie and fat gram that is eaten
- Dizziness and/or fainting spells
- Intense, dramatic mood swings
- An excessive need for control
- Wears loose clothing
- Exhaustion and fatigue
- Hides food in napkins, under beds, in drawers, etc.
- Abuses laxatives, diet pills, or diuretics
- Very poor self-esteem
- Complains of being cold
- Excessively and compulsively exercises
- Comes up with newfound excuses not to eat such as, "I already ate," and "I have an upset stomach"

- Tends to isolate in social situations or avoid social gathering
- Consumes a lot of non-caloric foods such as diet soda, gum, etc.
- Withdraws from touching others
- Avoids restaurants and eating in front of others
- Hair is falling out and/or becoming extremely dry and brittle
- Complexion has become pale and the skin is extremely dry
- Sees a distorted image of themselves in the mirror—like a "funhouse" mirror
- Meal times have become extremely ritualistic— e.g. the individual will insist on eating from the same bowl, cut food into tiny pieces, etc.
- Extremely defensive when questioned about weight
- Starts growing fine facial and body hair (lanugo)
- Hyperactivity

Bulimia Nervosa

- Bingeing and purging
- Severe self-criticism and poor self-esteem
- Feelings or expressions of guilt after eating
- Avoids eating in public or in front of others
- Excessive and compulsive exercise regimes
- Constant sore throat

- Broken blood vessels in eyes—i.e., bloodshot eyes
- Poor impulse control—i.e., drugs, alcohol, spending, mood, etc.
- Abuses laxatives, diet pills, ipecac, diuretics, and/or enemas
- Swollen glands in neck and puffiness in cheeks
- Often goes to the rest room right after meals and remains for an extended period of time
- Feels like they do not have control over food
- Hides food in secret locations for use during binges
- Eats a great deal but does not seem to gain or lose a lot of weight
- Has scrape wounds on the back of their knuckles (due to the contact between knuckles and teeth to induce vomiting)
- Extremely defensive when questioned about weight
- Tooth enamel is eroding and has increased cavities
- Has begun to wear extremely tight-fitting, figure-revealing clothes
- Constantly complains about being "fat," "obese," or "huge"
- Eats nothing or very little in front of others and then binges in private
- Quantities of food seem to mysteriously disappear from the refrigerator and/or pantry

- Tends to be sexually overactive, even quite promiscuous
- Takes numerous trips to grocery stores, convenience stores, etc. in a single day
- Has an enormous preoccupation with food and body weight
- Alternates between eating massive quantities of food and periods of self-starvation
- Goes through times of dramatic weight fluctuations of ten pounds or more within a short period of time
- Digestion problems
- Light bruising under the eyes and on the cheeks

BINGE-EATING DISORDER

- Rapid weight gain
- Eating large quantities of food even when not hungry
- Disgust and shame after overeating
- Eating food to the point that one is uncomfortable and even in pain
- Going from one diet to the next constantly
- Feeling out of control over food
- Eating late at night
- Hiding food around the home, anticipating the binge

- Does not use any measures (whatsoever) to purge the binged food
- Constant weight fluctuations
- Sexual avoidance
- Attributes any successes or failures to weight
- Main focus in life is food and weight
- Uses food to help cope with stress, emotional distress, and to overcome daily problems
- Eats nothing or very little in front of others, then binges in private—keeping a high weight
- Quantities of food seem to disappear from the refrigerator and/or pantry
- Believes that they will be a better person if/when they were thinner
- Resists activities due to shame that is affiliated with weight
- No longer feels full and/or satisfied when eating

eating disorder behaviors_____

While each eating disorder involves different behaviors, many of the root causes and issues are the same. Remember, the words "anorexia," "bulimia," and "binge-eating disorder" are simply categories the world has created to describe similar coping mechanisms surrounding food. So no matter the label, many of the associated behaviors are the same. Below is a list of commonly seen behaviors in anorexia, bulimia, and binge-eating disorder.

BEHAVIORS COMMONLY ASSOCIATED WITH EATING DISORDERS

- Frequent gazing in mirrors
- Discomfort when eating in front of other people
- Constant weighing, or avoiding of weighing
- Misperceptions of hunger, satiety, and other bodily functions
- Distorted body image
- Marked changes in personality, moods, or habits
- Preoccupation with exercise and/or exercising beyond exhaustion and physical limits
- Inability to concentrate
- Uses excessive amounts of condiments
- Eats spicy food often
- Stealing food
- Problems with interpersonal relationships (codependent or emotionally dependent)
- Obsessive-compulsive behavior (i.e., heating and reheating food, pulling out hair, hand washing, etc.)
- Difficulty sleeping, changes in sleeping patterns, fatigue
- Performance-based behavior
- Highly competitive

- Visiting websites that promote unhealthy ways to lose weight, reading books about weight loss and eating disorders

medical consequences _____

Eating disorders always involve abusing the body in some way—by starvation, overeating, or purging. This abuse may have long-lasting consequences on a person's physical health. Keep in mind that just as each individual may display different symptoms, different individuals may also have varied medical complications. Someone struggling with binge eating will have different medical needs than someone struggling with anorexia or bulimia. No matter what disorder or behaviors you are struggling with, they all can lead to death. In John 10:10, Jesus said, "The thief does not come except to steal, and to kill, and to destroy. I have come that they may have life, and that they may have it more abundantly" (NKJV). Below are examples of medical consequences of eating disorders.

- Low blood pressure/body temperature
- Hair loss
- Organ damage
- Osteoporosis
- Irregular heartbeat/heart failure

- Infertility
- Acid reflux
- Esophageal tears
- Constipation
- Anemia
- Loss of menstruation
- Leg and joint pain
- Decreased mobility due to weight gain (in binge-eating disorder)
- Excessive sweating and shortness of breath (in binge-eating disorder)
- Death

factors/root issues_____

Now that you are aware of the signs and symptoms of eating disorders, what are some of the factors that can contribute to eating disorders? Many, but not all, of these characteristics have to do with family dynamics. Common factors include:

- Societal and cultural values that promote slenderness as an important part of attractiveness
- Distorted body image and denial
- Using food as a reward or punishment
- Irrational beliefs and distorted thinking
- Perfectionism

- Low self-esteem
- Depression
- Control
- Dependency
- Distorted sexual identity
- Dysfunctional family system
- Performance pressure from family (especially with grades and other parent-approved activities)
- Involvement in activities which promote thinness for success, including athletic activities like dance, swimming, cheerleading, long-distance running, diving, gymnastics, ice skating, or activities that promote appearance over all other things, including modeling and beauty pageants

information for parents _____

FAMILY DYNAMICS

So what do you do if you suspect that your daughter has an eating disorder? The first step is to pray, and continually ask God to give you wisdom in handling the situation. Don't condemn her, but encourage her. She needs to know that you love her, no matter what she is doing. Use Jesus as an example. He never condemned. In fact, John 3:17 states, "For God did not send his Son into the world to condemn the world, but to save the world through Him" (NIV).

Offer to search for outside help. Many times, the parents are too emotionally involved and attached to offer objective help. Finding a great Christian counselor to guide the healing process is important. Just remember, Jesus is the answer to our problems, not a counselor. Make sure to find a counselor that will address the whole person—spirit, soul, and body.

> One of the most important aspects to remember is that it is not just the individual who is in need of help but the whole family!

Many times, overcoming an eating disorder involves help from a medical doctor, Christian psychologist, counselor, and a nutritionist. These people can be an important part of the healing process. But make sure that you find professionals who understand both the physical and spiritual aspects and are willing to locate the root causes of the eating disorder, instead of simply addressing the symptoms. Your goal for your daughter is a heart change, not simply good behavior. You want her to be free, accepting and loving herself the way she is, rather than living under self-imposed rules and regulations.

You, as a parent, also have a very important role in helping this healing process. We see several types of families in which eating disorders often emerge. One of the most important aspects to remember is that it is not just the individual who is in need of help but the whole family! It is important for the whole family to seek help together for whatever situations they are facing. One of the worst approaches parents can take is to be uninvolved in their child's life.

Frequently, these families have very similar characteristics. Almost every family dealing with eating disorders has one or more of the following: enmeshment, rigidity, overprotection, conflict avoidance, and an atmosphere of inconsistency and/or high expectations.

Enmeshment involves the blurring of parent/child boundaries, where personal information is shared in a "friendly" way, instead of keeping the parent/child roles separate. In a family experiencing rigidity, many times the parent(s) is very demanding and controlling, with the family following many spoken and unspoken rules. There is no room for questions, and most situations involve solutions only in perspectives of black and white. Overprotective parents may not allow a child to experience failure, even if it produces maturity. They are known to "jump" into situations in order to protect and save their child at any cost, keeping them from experiencing consequences.

Conflict avoidance is a common way for a family to deal with problematic and negative situations. The family may be living in denial or simply choosing to ignore any obvious problems that may "rock the boat." Inconsistency creates unpredictability, with parents not following through on promises, alternately praising and punishing a child for the same behaviors, and treating children differently in similar situations. Finally, many families that deal with eating disorders involve parents that put unreasonably high expectations on their children. This can include setting overly high standards for athletic, artistic, and academic performance, leading the child to feel that they are not accepted if they cannot meet these standards.

Many of these families often include a passive, uninvolved, overworking father and a controlling, overly involved mother. Sometimes the reverse of the same dynamic is present. Often, a girl may claim to be close to one parent, when actually, the relationship is superficial. This false closeness is often an attempt to cover up and deny underlying conflict.

Parents of a child struggling with an eating disorder often have similar characteristics, including:

- Not recognizing early signs until severe
- Seeing signs but believing it is a "phase"
- Involvement in their own crises, then displacing

all dysfunction and trauma onto their daughter
- Debilitation by their own struggles: chemical dependencies, mood disorders, or eating disorders, and are unable or unwilling to follow through on help for themselves

An eating disorder is not about food. There are many other factors that can lead to eating disorders. (See Appendix B for common eating disorder scenarios to learn of other factors related to family dynamics/situations.) Treating your child as if it is only about food is an example of denial.

As the parent of a child who has an eating disorder, balance is the key in handling the situation. A parent must be careful to act quickly and decisively yet not rush in and take control. If this balance is reached quickly and help is arranged, the chances of healing are greatly increased.

FATHERS

Fathers are so important in shaping their daughters' perceptions about being beautiful and loved. A father can be an influential factor in preventing an eating disorder in a daughter. There are many actions fathers can take to build positive, loving relationships with their daughters, thereby preventing eating disorders.

Focus on who your daughter is—what she says, believes, dreams, feels, and does—rather than how she looks. Speak words of affirmation to your daughter. Let her know how special and beautiful she is to you. Take her out for fun. Fathers have a profound influence on how their daughters view themselves. Focus on her uniqueness and treat her with respect. Your daughter is likely to choose a husband who acts like her father and has his values. Invest in her now to help your daughter choose someone who loves and respects her when she is an adult.

Enjoy sports and athletics with your daughter. Play catch, soccer, tag, jump rope, bike, or hike with her. Take her to sporting events you both enjoy. This helps her to learn all of the wonderful feats her body is capable of. This is also an important part of bonding with your daughter.

Get involved! Actively support and attend your daughter's activities, including school. Volunteer to chaperone, read to her class, coach, drive—you will make a difference!

As your daughter grows and matures, do not pull away from her out of fear. Many fathers do not know how to handle their daughter's budding sexuality. However, she needs you now, more than ever. Affirming her importance and identity will help her to become confident and comfortable as she becomes a young woman.

MOTHERS

Mothers and daughters have a special bond. Many mother-daughter relationships are loving and supportive. However, many problems can occur when mothers do not realize the profound effect they have on their daughter's development as a healthy young woman.

Set proper boundaries. Remember that your daughter is your child—not your best friend, sister, or mate. Many mothers attempt to live their lives through their daughters or try to be "best friends" with them. A myriad of problems can occur with this type of enmeshment. Most children are not emotionally equipped to deal with their mother's problems and emotions.

If you have more than one child, you already know that each of them has their own distinct personality. Be careful not to play favorites or compare one child to another. This can lead to extreme emotional damage, causing the children to try to "keep up" with the favored children, or causing the favored children to feel pressure to be perfect all the time.

While the next section is addressed to both parents, since both lead by example, a large majority of the issues apply to mothers. So, read carefully the following paragraphs and consider the kind of example you are for your children.

Lead by Example

An important fact to remember is that while most eating disorders usually develop during adolescence, a growing number of cases are occurring in very young children. Some of the girls we have seen at Mercy Ministries have exhibited signs and symptoms of eating disorders as young as three or four!

Children learn by example. Make sure that you try to maintain positive, healthy attitudes and behaviors toward your body. If your own thoughts about your body have been negative, it is time to check yourself! Your behavior and how you feel about your body also influences your child's beliefs. If you avoid activities, situations, and clothes because they call attention to your body or make you uncomfortable, your children may start to do the same thing.

Educate yourself about your body and then make sure to educate your daughter(s) about how the body works, how it grows, and how it goes through different stages in a person's life. In addition, affirm your daughter's femininity. Create an open dialogue— talk about the wonders of being a woman; invite your daughter to come to you with questions and feelings. Let her know she is loved. One of the scariest times for young girls is when their bodies go through puberty—hormonal changes can cause new, and many times uncomfortable, thoughts, attitudes, and feelings. This is a key time to instill positive beliefs about bodily changes and functions in your daughter in order to prevent the eating disorders that commonly begin during this time.

There are several positive actions that parents can take to educate their children about body image. Educate yourself and then your children about the dangers of trying to alter body size and shape through dieting. As far as food goes, make sure they eat a wide variety of foods for a balanced diet, consumed in at least three meals a day, around the same time each day. Never skip meals. Never force your child to "clean her plate"; this gives the child a sense of not being in control of her own food as well as possibly forcing her to eat when she is not hungry (this can destroy your child's ability to discern the feelings of hunger and fullness). The parent should decide what the menu is while the child determines the amount consumed. Avoid dividing foods into "good/bad, safe/unsafe, fattening/low-fat" categories.

Stress the importance of exercising for health, instead of for appearance. Help your children to make a commitment to exercise for these reasons also, instead of exercising in order to get rid of fat or compensating for the amount of calories they eat. Family cooperation and involvement in exercise activities help to foster positive attitudes about exercise. Try to fit exercise into family activities, such as riding bikes, going for walks or hikes, playing catch, etc.

Make sure that you practice not judging people by their appearance. Stress the importance of loving and accepting people for what they say, feel, and do—NOT by how thin or attractive they are.

What are your dreams and goals for your daughter? Do you overemphasize appearance? Be sure to avoid conveying an attitude that leads her to believe that you will love her more if she loses weight. Also choose your words wisely when talking to your children about their weight issues. If they are currently overweight, they are most likely already dealing with teasing, staring, shaming, and criticism from both family and peers. Shaming your child in an attempt to change her behavior will only intensify her desire to cope with negative situations through food. Decide what you can do to make sure you don't continually reinforce the idea that being larger or fatter than other children is *bad* and that smaller or thinner is *good*.

Many parents have said words or phrases that they did not even realize hurt their children so much. There are several common phrases that girls who have come to us at Mercy have pointed out as pivotal in the development of their eating disorder, for example, "Those pants make you look big." "Are you really going to eat all of that?" "You would be so much prettier if you lost a few pounds." These comments may lead your child to believe that because you feel this way about her, every adult feels this way about her. It is vital that your child feels safe at home and with you in order for her to begin to develop a healthy mindset and attitude about her body.

Overall, remember, *you* lead by example. It is your responsibility to be a good role model regarding not only body image but also sensible exercising, eating, and self-acceptance.

COMMUNICATION

Communication is a vital part to any relationship. You can't have one without the other. Many times, we have seen girls here at Mercy Ministries with eating disorders struggle in their family relationships. This struggle is partly due to communication barriers. These barriers can stem from fear of intimacy, family secrets, unspoken rules, avoidance, denial related to public image, and unhealthy family traditions of communication. How we communicate, either verbal or nonverbal, can also affect how the message comes across. The words we do or don't say always say something. You want to say what you mean to say, in love, and with the guidance of the Holy Spirit.

The ultimate goal in communicating with your loved one is to show that you love her unconditionally, are interested in her life, and that you will be there for her no matter what, while not enabling negative behaviors to continue. If this message is clearly related to your loved ones, they will sense an openness to come to you when they are afraid or in trouble.

Dos and Don'ts in Communication

Communication is a key factor in preventing eating disorders. Creating and maintaining open communication with your child is essential to foster a healthy relationship.

In order to keep a conversation going with your daughter, there are several actions you need to avoid. These are called communication blockers, and you need to be aware of them before opening up a dialogue with your child.

Interrupting can immediately end a conversation. When the speaker is cut off while talking, communication becomes impossible. Your child may feel that her thoughts and feelings are not important if she is continually cut off while speaking. As a result, they may become more hesitant to discuss difficulties with you. It is very important in a dialogue to make sure that both speakers have an opportunity to express themselves fully and openly.

Then, allowing both parties to express themselves fully and openly is not enough—it is important to actively listen while the other person is talking. Sometimes your loved one may just need to talk—not necessarily always receive your feedback. Simply listening to your child lets her know that you care about what she has to say, as well as communicating to her that her input and ideas are important.

Ignoring, sarcasm, name-calling, or insults will always have negative effects on communication and may, in fact, escalate the very conflict you are trying to avoid. Attaching labels or generalizing (i.e., "You always do this . . .") is a common trap to also avoid. Judging and blaming tends to put everything in terms of black and white, right and wrong.

> Simply listening to your child lets her know that you care about what she has to say.

Stating your opinion as fact may also end the discussion and/or escalate the conflict.

Open communication with your daughter is very important. For many people, this is not something that comes naturally. It may be uncomfortable when you begin to talk openly with your loved ones but know that it is essential and, as with any new skill, the more you practice, the better you will communicate. If this is a new idea for you, start small. For example, encourage your child to be aware of her feelings and to express them openly with you. Also, be willing to set an example by openly expressing your feelings to your child. Open communication between parents and children lowers the odds that your child's anxious or negative feelings will be repressed and expressed through food-related behaviors.

BUILDING SELF-ESTEEM AND IDENTITY

Building self-esteem in your child is an essential part of preventing an eating disorder. Children who have positive self-esteem are adept at expressing their feelings and are good problem solvers. They are less likely to succumb to peer and media pressures, food concerns and fears, body image issues, and disordered eating. Parents are responsible for building self-esteem in their child from birth on, and it is never too late to nurture self-esteem in your child! Tell them how loved they are, how unique and exceptional they are, how important they are to you, and most importantly, what God's Word says about them.

The basis of all self-esteem is knowing who you are in Christ, knowing the promises of God, and knowing His unconditional love. Simple ways to help develop this identity include educating yourself and your child about who God is and who you are in Him, studying the Bible, praying together, and having devotions as a family.

Another aspect of building your identity in Christ is replacing faulty thinking with God's truth, as mentioned previously (see Appendix A for further examples). If you hear your child engaging in critical self-talk, immediately help your child identify the lie and together find the truth in God's Word.

The following are several additional measures to help build self-esteem and identity:

- Spend quality time with your child; connect with her by finding ways to interact and engage her
- Provide your daughter with genuine connectedness and teach her meaningful life values
- Attend church together
- Be a trustworthy person
- Treat your daughter with respect; talk with her about her strengths
- Be a good listener; don't always give feedback (sometimes she just wants to be heard)
- Live out what you are asking of your daughter; do not follow the "do as I say, not as I do" mentality
- Love unconditionally
- Be a person of your word, even in disciplining your daughter
- Consistency breeds security, just as inconsistency breeds insecurity
- Emphasize enjoyment of the activity, rather than performance
- Encourage your child to take control of important aspects of her life and to make her own decisions

when appropriate; don't be afraid to provide
appropriate limits (being too limiting or allowing
the child too much freedom in her decisions can
be negative)

• Be an example of healthy, balanced, meaningful
living and problem solving; show your child
how to successfully resolve conflict

• Eat together as a family; this is a wonderful
time to find out about what is going on in your
daughter's life, as well as modeling healthy
eating behaviors

• Educate your child about media messages; do
not let her be exposed to weight-focused
programs or magazines

If you have discovered that there is still work to be
done to nurture your child's self-esteem, be comforted
that it is never too late to work on identity issues as a
family.

MY DAUGHTER HAS AN EATING DISORDER, NOW WHAT?

There are many dos and don'ts that are involved not
only in your child's healing process but also in your
family's. It is important that the parents and siblings
realize they have a role in the healing process.

Let's start with the "dos." One of the most important tools we use with the girls at Mercy is journaling. This allows the girls to track their thoughts, reactions, emotions, and possible responses. As a parent, you can do a type of journaling also. Start by writing down the specific behaviors and situations that you have observed and dealt with in your child. Write down how you dealt with the behavior as it happened and how it made you feel.

Your next step is to educate yourself and other family members about the eating disorder, which you are doing by reading this book. This will help you, as a concerned parent, to better understand the situation. Once you have a greater understanding of the nature of the disorder, you can be a more effective parent and decision-maker throughout the healing process.

It may be helpful for you, as a parent, to also seek guidance. Communicating with a Christian counselor or pastor helps you to process what your family is going through. An objective, listening ear may be able to point out things that you can do differently or show you ways you could possibly be contributing to your daughter's problem. It is important that you are open and teachable and that you seek the prayer and support that you need to maintain your relationship with God during this time.

Communication (both with your daughter and with those helping her) is a vital part of your daughter's healing process. Don't be afraid to speak up for what you know is right in the care of your daughter—especially if she is a minor. Exercise authority, responsibility, and wisdom in dealing with your daughter and those helping her.

Finally, patience is essential. Just as the eating disorder is a gradual process, the healing is also.

As with many things, the don'ts compile a much longer list. As the parent of a child struggling with an eating disorder, it is easy to blame yourself, your child, or any other number of persons for causing the eating disorder. Do not place blame! Concentrate on healing the root causes at this time. Parents can contribute to the healing process by having a positive attitude and getting the help and support you need for yourself.

Certain behaviors can be expected with eating disorders. To hide the behaviors and suffering for so long, a girl must become very adept at lying and manipulation. Do not allow your loved one to interrupt your life through manipulation, lying, arguing, guilt, threats, resentment, and bribes. In these situations, it is easy to "back off" for fear of your daughter's physical and emotional health becoming worse. This is exactly the opposite of what is needed! Decisive, clear, compassionate communication is necessary.

With clear communication, it is important to let your daughter know what is expected of her during this time. A major part of any eating disorder is control (as in your daughter's need to control every aspect of her life and those around her). As a parent, you are helping your daughter when you start to make decisions (therefore taking over control) about important (and not so important) issues, such as what to eat for dinner or where to go for vacation. In addition to taking back some control, make sure that you know what you are communicating with your words. Any blaming statements, such as, "Your illness is ruining our family," or "I can't take much more of this," will make the child feel as if she is in charge of the family's well-being, causing her to be even angrier, possibly furthering the problem. Other statements, such as, "What can I do to help?" also make the person struggling with an eating disorder feel as if she has to take charge and then feel like more of a failure when she cannot answer.

PRAYERS AND CONFESSIONS

At Mercy Ministries, we have found that a person walks out what she believes. We desire to give you the tools to influence your life or the life of your loved one in a positive way, thereby bringing complete healing. As mentioned before, aligning your conversation with what God says brings a positive change to your situation (Rom. 10:17).

Also, as previously stated, it is important to speak these prayers and declarations aloud, as "Life and death are in the power of the tongue" (Prov. 18:21). The following prayers and confessions are designed to be used by parents for themselves and to speak over their children.

Prayers for Parents

Lord Jesus, I ask you to bless my daughter, _____. I pray that you would lead by your Holy Spirit and show her Your way. I surrender this situation to You and ask You to do Your work in my daughter. Give me strength and wisdom that I may be led by Your Spirit concerning my daughter's welfare. In Jesus' name, Amen.

God, I come to you with a heart of surrender concerning my daughter, _____. I worry about her at times and I need to know I can release these cares upon You and You will take these worries. Protect her and guide her. Give me wisdom to know what to say and to do what's best for my daughter. In Your name, Amen.

Lord, I repent of any action or behavior that has contributed to my daughter's eating disorder. Holy

Spirit, reveal to me any changes I need to make to help me be a better parent. In Jesus' name, Amen.

For Parents To Speak Over Their Children

1. _____ will be free from worry concerning what she will eat or drink because Jesus knows her needs and will provide what she needs (Matt. 6:25–33).

2. _____ is an overcomer (1 John 5:4–5).

3. Father in heaven, I thank you that every member of _____'s body is yielded to you as an instrument of righteousness (Rom. 6:13).

4. _____ will know the truth, and the truth will set her free (John 8:32).

5. I pray the depths of her heart be flooded with light so she can know and understand the hope to which she is called (Eph. 1:18).

6. I pray that she may really come to know (through experience for herself) the love of Christ, which far surpasses mere knowledge, that she may be filled (through all her being) unto all the fullness of God

(may have the richest measure of the divine presence and become a body wholly filled and flooded with God Himself!) (Eph. 3:19).

7. _____ has strength for all things in Christ who empowers her (she is ready for anything and to do anything through Him who infuses inner strength unto her) (Phil. 4:13).

8. _____ shall not die but live and shall declare the works and recount the illustrious acts of the Lord (Ps. 118:17).

9. Lord, I speak over _____'s life that You are her strength and song and You have become her salvation (Ps. 118:14).

10. And the Spirit of the Lord shall rest upon _____; the Spirit of wisdom and understanding, the Spirit of counsel and might, the Spirit of knowledge and of the reverential and obedient fear of the Lord. And she shall not judge by the sight of her eyes, neither decide by the hearing of her ears (Isa. 11:2–3).

If you are a parent whose daughter is struggling with an eating disorder, please know there is hope, there is help, and there is a God who is bigger than all of what you are facing.

Just because your daughter needs help doesn't mean you have been a bad parent. Life is filled with trouble and problems, but God is available to help us face and overcome the problems of life, if we call upon Him.

If you are the one who is struggling with an eating disorder, it is my prayer that by now you realize there is hope, there is healing, and freedom is possible. The same freedom Laura and the other girls are experiencing is also available to you.

laura's epilogue

You have just finished reading my story. This is my heart and soul, feelings and thoughts poured out on paper. It is very personal and intimate. I was willing to include my story in this book for two reasons. I wanted people to see exactly how devastating and life-consuming an eating disorder is. To walk in my shoes, through the journal entries, you were able to feel and experience the agony of this obsession. I also wanted you to know that an eating disorder does not have to be a life sentence.

I was not hand-chosen by God to be the only person to overcome an eating disorder. Freedom is available for anyone, and the principles of the path of freedom are found in this book. If you make the decision, and choose to listen to God, you too can overcome an eating disorder. I had to choose to think differently, live differently, and submit my life in complete surrender. This was not easy, but it is possible.

My passion now is that everyone knows the truth about eating disorders. Eating disorders are not life-long, incurable diseases. It is possible to be free, to not think food thoughts all day and night, or obsess over weight and calories.

Make the choice today to begin your path to freedom. It is worth it. I know. I am living proof.

replacing lies
with truth

As discussed earlier, one part of the healing process is to replace lies with truth. These are Laura's ungodly beliefs—the lies she had been believing about herself. After acknowledging these lies, she searched the Bible to find what God's Word said that contradicted the lies she believed about herself. This is an individual process—as everyone has different thoughts that they must take captive and submit to God as part of the process of renewing their minds. This practice is a necessary step in overcoming eating disorders. If you only apply one thing from this book to your life—let it be this! You must identify the lies you believe about yourself and replace them with God's truth!

Ungodly Belief: I am unlovable and unworthy. If you knew the real me, you would reject me. No one really likes me.

Godly Belief: With God's help, I will learn to be myself and trust Him to bring people into my life that will appreciate me and respect me for who I am. My worth is in who God says I am.

> *But the very hairs of your head are all numbered. Do not fear therefore; you are of more value than many sparrows* (Luke 12:7 NKJV).

> *For he made Him who knew no sin to be sin for us, that we might become the righteousness of God in Him* (2 Cor. 5:21 NKJV).

> *To the praise of the glory of His grace, by which He made us accepted in the Beloved. In Him we have redemption through His blood, the forgiveness of sins, according to the riches of His grace* (Eph. 1:6–7 NKJV).

Ungodly Belief: Even when I do my best, it is not good enough. I can never meet the standard.

Godly Belief: I am fully loved, completely accepted, and totally pleasing to God. Regardless of how much I do or fail to do, I will remain fully loved, completely accepted, and totally pleasing to God. I choose to surrender to Him, trusting my faith in Him and His ability to sustain me. I will seek to be a God-pleaser, not a people-pleaser.

The steps of a good man are ordered by the Lord, and He delights in his way. Though he fall, he shall not be utterly cast down; for the Lord upholds him with His hand (Ps. 37:23–24 NKJV).

I can do all things through Christ who strengthens me (Phil. 4:13 NKJV).

But seek first the kingdom of God and His righteousness, and all these things shall be added to you (Matt. 6:33 NKJV).

Ungodly Belief: I must be passive in order to avoid conflict that would risk others' disapproval of me. No one will like me if I confront them or "rock the boat."

Godly Belief: I choose to trust God to take care of me when conflicts arise. He will teach me to handle situations of conflict in a godly manner.

The fear of man brings a snare, but whoever trusts in the Lord shall be safe (Prov. 29:25 NKJV).

When a man's ways please the Lord, He makes even his enemies to be at peace with him (Prov. 16:7 NKJV).

Do not be afraid of their faces, for I am with you to deliver you, says the Lord. Then the Lord put forth His

hand and touched my mouth and the Lord said to me:
I have put My words in your mouth (Jer. 1:8–9 NKJV).

Ungodly Belief: I am unattractive. It is impossible to lose weight. I am just stuck. I am fat, ugly, and will always be that way no matter what.

Godly Belief: God made me and He loves me. He accepts me just like I am, yet He will help me with any changes that will improve my health and lengthen my life. I choose to love myself and value myself by God's standards and realize that my completion as a woman comes from my Creator.

I beseech you, therefore, brethren by the mercies of God that you present your bodies as a living sacrifice, holy, acceptable to God, which is your reasonable service. And do not be conformed to this world, but be transformed by the renewing of your mind, that you may prove what is that good and acceptable and perfect will of God (Rom. 12:1–2 NKJV).

The Lord has appeared of old to me, saying, "Yes, I have loved you with an everlasting love; Therefore, with lovingkindness I have drawn you" (Jer. 31:3 NKJV).

Jesus said, "If you can believe, all things are possible to him who believes" (Mark 9:23 NKJV).

Therefore, I say to you, whatever things you ask, when you pray believe that you receive them, and you will have them (Mark 11:24 NKJV).

And you are complete in Him, who is the head of all principality and power (Col. 2:10 NKJV).

Ungodly Belief: I will always be insecure and fearful. I am a bad person.

Godly Belief: I can be confident in Him who created me. I will draw my security, courage, and identity from what God says about me.

For God has not given us a spirit of fear, but of power and of love and of a sound mind (2 Tim. 1:7 NKJV).

You are of God, little children, and you have overcome them: for He who is in you is greater than he who is in the world (1 John 4:4 NKJV).

This Book of the Law shall not depart from your mouth, but you shall meditate in it day and night, that you may observe to do according to all that is written in it. For then you will make your way prosperous, and then you will have good success. Have I not commanded you? Be strong and of good courage; do not be afraid, nor be dismayed, for the Lord your

God is with you wherever you go (Josh. 1:8–9 NKJV).

There is no fear in love; but perfect love casts out fear, because fear involves torment. But he who fears has not been made perfect in love (1 John 4:18 NKJV).

Ungodly Belief: I have wasted a lot of time and energy, some of my best years. Turmoil is normal for me.

Godly Belief: God will restore all the time I have wasted or was lost by my choices or by the choices of others. God gives me peace.

So I will restore to you the years that the swarming locust has eaten, the crawling locust, and the chewing locust . . . (Joel 2:25 NKJV).

You will keep him in perfect peace, whose mind is stayed on You, because he trusts in You (Isa. 26:3 NKJV).

Be anxious for nothing, but in everything by prayer and supplication, with thanksgiving, let your requests be made known to God; and the peace of God, which surpasses all understanding, will guard your hearts and minds through Christ Jesus. Finally, brethren, whatever things are true, whatever things are noble, whatever things are just, whatever things are pure, whatever things are lovely, whatever things are of good report, if there is any virtue and if there is anything praiseworthy—meditate on these things (Phil. 4:6–8 NKJV).

Peace I leave with you, My peace I give to you; not as the world gives do I give to you. Let not your heart be troubled, neither let it be afraid (John 14:27 NKJV).

To all who mourn in Israel He will give: Beauty for ashes; Joy instead of mourning; Praise instead of heaviness. For God has planted them like strong and graceful oaks for His own glory (Isa. 61:3 LB).

Ungodly Belief: I will always have financial problems. I will never be able to get ahead.

Godly Belief: I will be responsible for my choices and spending decisions. I will be a good steward with my money and be wise in my spending. Because I will tithe and become a giver, God will see to it that my finances come into order.

Blessed is the man who walks not in the counsel of the ungodly, nor stands in the path of sinners, nor sits in the seat of the scornful; but his delight is in the law of the Lord, and in His law he meditates day and night. He shall be like a tree planted by the rivers of water, that brings forth its fruit in its season, whose leaf also shall not wither; and whatever he does shall prosper (Ps. 1:1–3 NKJV).

I have been young, and now am old; yet I have not seen the righteous forsaken, nor his descendants begging bread. He is ever merciful, and lends; and his descendants are blessed (Ps. 37:25–26 NKJV).

Give, and it will be given to you: good measure, pressed down, shaken together, and running over will be put into your bosom. For with the same measure that you use, it will be measured back to you (Luke 6:38 NKJV).

"Bring all the tithes into the storehouse, that there may be food in my house, and try me now in this," says the Lord of hosts, "If I will not open the windows of heaven and pour out for you such blessing that there will not be room enough to receive it. And I will rebuke the devourer for your sakes, so that he will not destroy the fruit of your ground, nor shall the vine fail to bear fruit for you in the field," says the Lord of hosts (Mal. 3:10–11 NKJV).

He who is faithful in a very little [thing] is faithful also in much, and he who is dishonest and unjust in a very little [thing] is dishonest and unjust also in much (Luke 16:10 AMP).

Ungodly Belief: I always make wrong decisions. I am unable to take care of myself or make wise decisions. I am out there all alone.

Godly Belief: I choose to believe that God will help me to make wise decisions as I ask Him for direction for my life. If I align my decisions with the Word of God, I will consistently make the right choice. God will protect and keep me.

If any of you lacks wisdom, let him ask of God, who gives to all liberally, without reproach, and it will be given to him (James 1:5 NKJV).

Call to me, and I will answer you, and show you great and mighty things, which you do not know (Jer. 33:3 NKJV).

Your Word is a lamp to my feet and a light to my path (Ps. 119:105 NKJV).

Trust in the Lord with all your heart, and lean not on your own understanding; in all your ways acknowledge Him, and He shall direct your paths (Prov. 3:5–6 NKJV).

My sheep hear My voice, and I know them, and they follow Me. And I give them eternal life, and they shall never perish; neither shall anyone snatch them out of my hand. My Father, who has given them to Me, is greater than all; and no one is able to snatch them out of My Father's hand (John 10:27–28 NKJV).

Let your character or moral disposition be free from love of money [including greed, avarice, lust, and craving for earthly possessions] and be satisfied with your present [circumstances and with what you have]; for He [God] Himself has said, I will not in any way fail you nor give you up nor leave you without support. [I will] not, [I will] not, [I will] not in any degree leave you helpless nor forsake nor let [you] down (relax My hold on you)! [Assuredly not!] (Heb. 13:5 AMP).

If you abide in me, and my words abide in you, you will ask what you desire, and it shall be done for you (John 15:7).

Ungodly Belief: If I let anyone get close to me, I may get my heart broken again. I can't let myself risk it.

Godly Belief: God will heal every hurt in my heart. He will give me wisdom in relationships and show me when I can share my heart.

The Spirit of the Lord God is upon Me, because the Lord has anointed Me to preach good tidings to the poor; He has sent Me to heal the brokenhearted, to proclaim liberty to the captives, and the opening of the prison to those who are bound (Isa. 61:1 NKJV).

Keep your heart with all diligence, for out of it spring the issues of life (Prov. 4:23 NKJV).

Set your mind on things above, not on things on the earth. For you died, and your life is hidden with Christ in God (Col. 3:2–3 NKJV).

Now may the God of peace Himself sanctify you completely; and may your whole spirit, soul, and body be preserved blameless at the coming of our Lord Jesus Christ. He who calls you is faithful, who also will do it (1 Thess. 5:23–24 NKJV).

Brethren, I do not count myself to have apprehended; but one thing I do, forgetting those things which are behind and reaching forward to those things which are ahead. I press toward the goal for the prize of the upward call of God in Christ Jesus (Phil. 3:13–14 NKJV).

Now to Him who is able to do exceedingly abundantly above all that we ask or think, according to the power that works in us, to Him be glory in the church by Christ Jesus to all generations, forever and ever. Amen (Eph. 3:20 NKJV).

Ungodly Belief: I can't understand God.

Godly Belief: With the help of the Holy Spirit and His Word, I can understand God. My relationship with God will grow stronger, and I will be able to hear Him more clearly.

For "who has known the mind of the Lord that he may instruct Him?" But we have the mind of Christ (1 Cor. 2:16 NKJV).

The entrance of Your words gives light; it gives understanding to the simple (Ps. 119:130 NKJV).

That the God of our Lord Jesus Christ, the Father of glory, may give to you the spirit of wisdom and revelation in the knowledge of Him, the eyes of your understanding being enlightened; that you may know what is the hope of His calling, what are the riches of the glory of His inheritance in the saints, and what is the exceeding greatness of His power toward us who believe, according to the working of His mighty power (Eph. 1:17–19 NKJV).

Seeing then that we have a great High Priest who has passed through the heavens, Jesus the Son of God, let us hold fast our confession. For we do not have a High Priest who cannot sympathize with our weaknesses, but was in all points tempted as we are, yet without sin. Let us therefore come boldly to the throne of grace, that we may obtain mercy and find grace to help in time of need (Heb. 4:14–16 NKJV).

For this purpose was the Son of God manifested, that He might destroy the works of the devil (1 John 3:8 NKJV).

For God so loved the world that He gave His only begotten Son, that whoever believes in Him should not perish but have everlasting life. For God did not send His son into the world to condemn the world, but that the world through Him might be saved (John 3:16–17 NKJV).

Ungodly Belief: I will always be lonely. The special man in my life will not be there for me.

Godly Belief: God said He sets the solitary in families. I choose to believe that He will see to it that I will always belong to a family and have friends if I show myself friendly. I choose to believe that God is preparing the man He wants in my life just as He is preparing me. He will give me discernment to know which man He has prepared for me to marry and how to share myself with him in a godly manner.

God sets the lonely in families, he leads forth the prisoners with singing; but the rebellious live in a sun-scorched land (Ps 68:6 NIV).

A man who has friends must himself be friendly, but there is a friend who sticks closer than a brother (Prov. 18:24 NKJV).

Delight yourself also in the Lord, and He shall give you the desires of your heart. Commit your way to the Lord, trust also in Him, and He shall bring it to pass (Ps. 37:4–5 NKJV).

eating disorder
scenarios

The following scenarios are common to many of the girls that have come to Mercy Ministries for help. Although we have talked about specific causes and behaviors that can lead to disorders, we wanted to present the following scenarios to help you understand the struggles that many families deal with in these situations.

I MUST BE FAT AND UGLY

Stephanie's dad loves to joke and tease his daughter, as he has done since she was young, but lately she does not seem to respond in the same laughing way she used to. In talking to a close friend, she confides: "My dad is always joking like, 'you don't need that extra chip now do you,' or 'you

better watch out or those pants will get too tight'—
I mean I just feel so fat and ugly when he says that.
If my dad thinks I'm fat, every guy must think I'm
just huge." She buys diet pills on her way home
from school.

You can see how these comments and this situation
can cause the daughter to believe the lie, "If my dad
thinks I'm this fat, every guy must think I'm huge!"
Her immediate solution for the lie was to buy diet
pills to try to make herself feel accepted and attractive. At Mercy, we have seen that the use of diet pills
can lead to abuse, not only of the diet pills, but also
laxatives and diuretics, as many as fifty to one
hundred a day.

CONFRONTING THE DECEPTION

Jackie's friends have begun to notice that she "disap-
pears" to the bathroom as soon as they finish their
meals. She just dismisses it as "I always have to go as
soon as I eat," but something about that just doesn't
sit right. They wonder if they should say something
or if it's nothing and they would just embarrass themselves for bringing it up.

This behavior is consistent with the purging seen in
bulimia nervosa. Women who are engaged in

purging their food often exhibit signs of deception and use many excuses to cover their behavior, often destroying social and family relationships. Although it may feel uncomfortable, it is up to friends and family to address the situation with love and concern for the safety of their loved one.

TAKING NOTICE OF BEHAVIOR

Parents have begun to notice that their daughter always seems to be cold lately. Even though it's late spring, she is still wearing baggy sweatshirts and long pants. She always has on socks and is usually wearing a sweater or some other kind of layered clothing. Now that they have begun to notice, her clothes just don't seem to fit right and always look baggy on her.

They are also beginning to notice that their daughter may be hiding food during meals rather than eating it. Frequently, large "crumbs" of food are on the floor around where she sits. No one sees her eating, yet suddenly her plate is basically empty of food and she will excuse herself. The mother has noticed food falling out of folded napkins as she does laundry and has, on occasion, found pieces of food in her pockets. The last time her mother was in her room looking for something, she noticed a bag in the corner of the room. As she looked, the bag was full of discarded food items.

The positive aspect of this situation is that the parents have started to take notice of their daughter's behavior, consistent with the behaviors of those struggling with anorexia nervosa. Most likely, these behaviors began long ago and have now progressed to the point that the parents can no longer ignore their daughter's cries for help, such as leaving physical evidence of her struggle (bag on the floor, etc.).

THE BULIMIA PROGRESSES

A mother is repulsed and disgusted while cleaning her daughter's room. She had noticed a smell coming from her room but dismissed it since her daughter is a bit on the "disorganized" side. When she decides to clean the room to surprise her daughter, she finds several folded paper bags throughout the room—in the closet, under the bed, behind some books. The mother looks inside and is shocked to find what looks like vomit.

Many times, as bulimia progresses, a person will resort to bingeing and purging any place she can. This includes not only purging in the bathroom, but as seen above, in paper bags, in closets, in pockets, in jars, etc.

EXCESSIVE EXERCISE

A college girl notices that every time she sees her friend, she is either walking or doing sit-ups and crunches, even while they are socializing. She skips meals, preferring to go to the gym rather than eat and spend time with friends. Last week, she went by the laundry room and her friend was doing push-ups in front of the washing machine.

Many people with an eating disorder will exercise excessively in an attempt to burn calories. They often attempt to hide their exercise habits out of shame.

BINGEING AND WEIGHT GAIN

An adult child comes home to visit her family. They notice she has gained a significant amount of weight since they last saw her, and they are becoming concerned about her health. At family mealtimes, they notice she not only eats seconds but also seems to eat more quickly than others and takes unusually large bites of her food. She tends to "graze" throughout the day, wandering into the kitchen to see what there is to eat. She prepares elaborate or large meals for herself and others at every meal. She also doesn't act like herself—she is usually quite interactive but now seems to prefer being alone or watching television.

When people think of the term "eating disorder," they often think of an extremely thin, emaciated person. However, many girls who suffer from these disorders oftentimes *gain* weight during their struggle (binge eaters, bulimics). Many people do not realize that binge eating is also considered an eating disorder and has similar root issues and causes as anorexia and bulimia.

acknowledgments

The highest honor to Jesus Christ—
The one and only life changer.

A very special thank-you to Laura Schultz for the courage to lay open her heart and life in great detail so that others can experience freedom. Also, thank you for the countless number of hours you spent both in writing and editing. Only eternity will reveal the impact of your labor of love.

To Kristy, Lisa, and Jenny—Thank you for allowing your stories to be told so that others can have hope.

To Amy Gilbert, my personal assistant—Thank you for loving so unconditionally, and for your many hours of serving and giving. Your value is beyond human measure.

To all Mercy Staff—Thank you for serving, giving, and loving the girls every day. Because you are called, God has equipped you. Thank you for being willing and obedient to fulfill your assignments. Without you, there would be no stories to write about.

To our supporters—You are a part of every changed life because of your financial help. Thank you for your generosity and compassion.

To Joyce Meyer—Thank you for being such a Godly role model and for your example of honesty, integrity, and faithfulness. Thank you for giving of yourself in every way.

To Point of Grace—Denise, Heather, Shelley, and Terry, I thank God for putting us together—your hearts are so beautiful! Thank you for providing a platform to share Mercy Ministries. Multitudes of lives have been impacted because of your involvement.

To Mark and Darlene Zschech—Thank you for your awesome friendship, and for partnering with us to make Mercy Australia a reality.

To Sue Semrau—Thank you for providing a solitary place for me to put these words on paper.

To Dr. Linda Mintle—A special thank-you for lending your expertise to our counselors as a friend and supporter of Mercy Ministries. (Dr. Mintle's website is www.drlindahelps.com.)

resources

Bevere, Lisa. *Out of Control and Loving It!* Lake Mary, Fla.: Creation House, 1996.

Bevere, Lisa. *The True Measure of a Woman: You Are More Than What You See.* Lake Mary, Fla.: Creation House, 1997.

Bevere, Lisa. *You Are Not What You Weigh: Escaping the Lie and Living the Truth.* Lake Mary, Fla.: Creation House, 1998.

Capps, Charles. *God's Creative Power.* Tulsa, Okla.: Harrison House, 1976.

Cloud, Henry and John Townsend. *Boundaries.* Grand Rapids, Mich.: Zondervan, 1992.

Hilton, Melody. *Double Honor: Uprooting Shame in Your Life.* Elizabethville, Pa.: Double Honor Ministries, 1999.

Homme, Martha. *Seeing Your Loved One in God's Image.* Chattanooga, Tenn.: Turning Point, 2001.

Homme, Martha. *Seeing Yourself in God's Image.* Chattanooga, Tenn.: Turning Point, 1998.

Keller, Kay, et al. *Hand in Hand: Devotions for Encouraging Families Through the Pain of a Daughter with an Eating Disorder.* Phoenix, Ariz.: Ironwood Lithographers, 1998.

McGee, Robert. *The Search for Significance.* Nashville, Tenn.: Word Publishing, 1998.

Meyer, Joyce. *Eat and Stay Thin.* Tulsa, Okla.: Harrison House, 1999.

Meyer, Joyce. *How to Succeed at Being Yourself: Finding the Confidence to Fulfill Your Destiny.* Tulsa, Okla.: Harrison House, 1999.

Meyer, Joyce. *Managing Your Emotions.* Tulsa, Okla.: Harrison House, 1997.

Minirth, Frank and Les Carter. *The Anger Workbook.* Nashville, Tenn.: Thomas Nelson, 1993.

The following websites may contain information contrary to the beliefs and values of Nancy Alcorn and Mercy Ministries of America. Mercy Ministries of America does not neccessarily endorse all the information given on the following websites.

WEBSITE MATERIAL

www.raphacare.com
www.edreferral.com
www.drlindahelps.com
www.something-fishy.org
www.anonymousone.com
www.eatingdisorderinfo.org